How to Build in the Country

Good Advice from the Past on How to Choose a Site, Plan, Design, Build, Decorate & Landscape Your Country Home

THANK You!

Edited By Donald J. Berg, AIA

ISBN 0-9663075-1-8
Library of Congress
Catalog Card Number: 98-093982
Copyright 1999 by Donald J. Berg

Published by:

DJB

Donald J. Berg, AIA
PO Box 698, Rockville Centre, NY 11571
516 766-5585

This is a revised and enlarged edition of the book originally published by Antiquity Reprints in 1985 and Ten Speed Press in 1986.

CONTENTS

4

About This Book

The builders, architects and landscapers of last century's picture-perfect country homes left us a legacy of design ideas and practical building advice. Their words and drawings are as valuable now as they were when they were penned.

I've selected some of the best hints from nineteenth century builders' guides, farm journals and home and garden magazines. I've used some of them myself and made mistakes enough to know that I should have used more.

The book follows a complete building sequence from first choosing a site through final furnishing and planting. I hope you enjoy your reading and, if you're dreaming of building a home in the country, that the ideas are of some help. - Don Berg

Thanks

This is a new edition of a book that was first published by Antiquity Reprints and then by Ten Speed Press. I'd like to thank John Moses for his help with the original design and typography and all of the folks at Ten Speed Press for the great job they did on their edition.

My wife Christine was kind enough to take time out of her busy schedule to edit all the text and to help make a little sense out of my babble.

I appreciate my daughter Bethany's and my son Christopher's patience with me as I missed parts of another holiday season to get this done.

In particular, I have to thank my son Ted for encouraging me to revise and reissue this book. Like the sage advice you'll find in the text, his idea made perfect sense: "Dad, do *How to Build In the Country* again. People liked it the first time, and let's face it, you don't have that many good ideas."

Foreword

By architect Calvert Vaux, from his 1867 book, *Villas & Cottages*

"Almost every American has an equally unaffected, though not, of course, an equally appreciative, love for 'the country.' This love appears intuitive, and the possibility of ease and a country place or suburban cottage, large or small, is a vision that gives a zest to the labors of industrious thousands. This one simple fact is of marked importance; it shows that there is an innate homage to the natural in contradistinction to the artificial—a preference for the works of God to the works of man; and no matter what passing influences may prevent the perfect working of this tendency, there it exists; and with all its town-bred incongruities and frequently absurd short-comings, it furnishes a valuable proof of inherent good, true, and healthy taste."

Country home design, from an 1888 issue of the magazine *Shoppell's Modern Houses*

First Floor Plan

Second Floor Plan

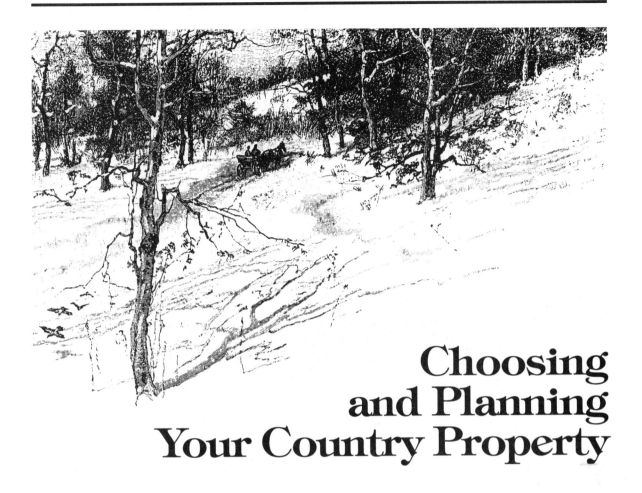

Choosing and Planning Your Country Property

The first step to having a great country place is to find a great site. Here's what yesterday's builders looked for in their property and how they planned their buildings on that land.

Find a Waterside Site If You Can

A.J.Downing, *Hints to Persons About Building in the Country*, 1847

"Those valleys bordering on large pieces of water, which maintain a more uniform temperature than the land, afford admirable sites for building. Such are the valleys of large rivers and lakes, like the Hudson, and the great lakes in the State of New York. These broad sheets of water have such an effect in equalizing the temperature of the atmosphere for miles around them, that they usually add a month or more to the growing season on their banks. The frosts of Spring and Autumn are warded off, and crops of fruit are preserved, when they are destroyed in the interior of the country. On the banks of a large bay in the Hudson, the spring is always ten days earlier, and the autumn ten days later, than in the same latitude thirty miles east or west. The shores of lakes Ontario, Erie, and the smaller lakes in this State, which do not freeze in winter, enjoy a still more marked exception from destructive frosts, as compared with the back districts of country unprotected by them. Every person choosing a site for a country residence, who is fond of his garden and orchard, will, therefore, when he has it in his power, give the preference to the borders of large rivers and lakes."

"There are many beautiful, tempting, and, we may add, many really excellent sites in valleys. The soil is usually fertile, and the growth luxuriant. But the usual objections to narrow and deep valleys, where there is much water, are the dampness, and, often, the unhealthiness, of the air there.

There is also another point worthy the consideration of our readers. This is the coldness in winter of all small or deep valleys, compared with the surrounding country. This, though not very perceptible to the senses, exerts a very important influence on vegetation. In a quiet winter night, the coldest air slides down into the bottoms of valleys, while the hills around are in a considerably higher temperature. Hence, many trees and plants will thrive on a higher level, which perish in a deep valley. We know a charming valley in Connecticut, where the peach and the cherry seldom perfect a crop of fruit, owing to the greater severity and prevalence of the frosts there, while they bear uniformly and well, in the adjacent country, on a higher level."

Avoid Cold Valleys

A.J.Downing, *Hints to Persons About Building in the Country*, 1847

Don't Build on Bad Soil

A.J.Downing, *Hints to Persons About Building in the Country*, 1847

"In choosing a position for the house itself, the character of the soil and sub-soil should receive attention. It is evident on a moment's reflection, that the worst soil is one naturally wet, and the best, one naturally dry. The site for a dwelling should never be selected where the sub-soil is naturally wet and springy, unless it is capable of being made perfectly dry by draining - because dampness of the house, and consequent unhealthiness of its inmates, almost inevitably follow the selection of such a situation. A good loam soil, on a gravely sub-soil, is always an unexceptionable position for placing a house, as far as relates to this point. To those who desire fine ornamental grounds, or even fertile meadows and orchards (and we can hardly imagine the case of any country proprietor who does not), of course, attention to the quality of the soil immediately about the site of the house will not be overlooked. Though it is not impossible to render almost any soil fit for cultivation, yet it is infinitely wiser to chose a site where nature had given the necessary conditions of good soil, rather than to undertake the great labor and ill-rewarded expense attending all considerable operations to change the character of soil."

Don't Build on Top of a Hill

A.J.Downing, *Hints to Persons About Building in the Country*, 1847

"The most popular sites, those usually chosen by inexperienced proprietors in the middle States, are the summits of hills of moderate elevation, overlooking extensive prospects. Now there are some advantages, but also very great disadvantages, in these high positions. The prominent advantages which such sites are supposed to possess are wide prospects, and consciousness for the dwelling itself: to see, and to be seen, to the greatest possible advantage. But every one having a cultivated taste for fine landscapes, must greatly prefer agreeable views, vistas of portions of trees with rich foreground, to wide panoramas of country. It is, in fact, the difference between a pictured landscape, and a geographical map. The panorama is striking and interesting, when seen occasionally, but it wants the interest, the home-like feeling of appropriation - which a view of moderate extent affords. As regards the ambition which is gratified with placing one's house where it may be a landmark for ten miles round, it is a false ambition which we have no sympathy with - a taste not in keeping with our social habits, and foreign to that equality of condition which all Americans are impatient of seeing greatly violated.

There are practical objections to sites upon the tops of hills, or high ridges, which are of great moment. The first of these is the great difficulty of raising all kinds of trees and shrubs in high and exposed sites. There are, apparently, but few persons aware that ornamental trees will advance twice as rapidly, the soil being the same, in a midway level, or a valley, as they will upon the summits of hills or high ridges. This is partly owing to the high winds, to which they are constantly exposed, and which render the annual growth of wood comparatively dwarfish, and partly to the greater dryness of the soil, which, in this climate, does not afford a continued supply of moisture to the roots.

But we may also add, as an offset to the grand prospect which these elevated sites afford, the labor of walking, riding, or driving up and down a long hill. If the road can be made gradual and easy this is not much, but in situations that we could name, where this is by no means the case, the daily effort (for there is no escape from it), of dragging up and down hill, becomes a burden, to be relieved of which, the proprietor would gladly exchange his wide-spread view for a more limited landscape, and an easier approach."

Build Your Home Away from the Road

E.H.Leland, *Farm Homes,* 1882

"The building site is, of course, the first thing to be considered. One's first resolution regarding it should be to avoid all anxiety to jump into the road. A house crowding upon the highway loses all dignity and home-like repose, and gains nothing but dust. Such choice of location may possibly be an hereditary trait, coming down from that long ago time, when houses grew up along the faintly-marked trails of emigration, and closely clung there, as if in mortal fear of savages and wild animals lurking in the back-ground. But in these peaceful days, it is in better taste to sit back in a leisurely and composed way, as if not afraid of one's own fields and woodlands, but at home and happy with them. Let no site be chosen because of its proximity to the road, or because it is "handy to water." Select the finest spot on the farm - a place combining, if possible, elevation, eastern and southern frontage, natural trees, a pleasant outlook, and make all else conform to it."

Plan Your Entry Drive

Calvert Vaux, *Villas & Cottages,* 1867

"In a case that recently occurred near a country town at some distance from New York, a road was run through a very beautiful estate, one agreeable feature of which was a pretty though small pond that, even in the dryest seasons, was always full of water, and would have formed an agreeable adjunct to a country-seat. A single straight pencil-line on the plan doubtless marked out the direction of the road; and as this line happened to go straight through the pond, straight through the pond was the road accordingly carried, the owner of the estate personally superintending the operation, and thus spoiling his sheet of water, diminishing the value of his lands, and increasing expense by the cost of filling in, without any advantage whatever: for a winding road so laid out as to skirt the pond, would have been far more attractive and agreeable than the harsh, straight line that is now scored like a railway track clear through the undulating surface of the property; and such barbarisms are of constant occurrence. Points of this nature deserve the utmost attention, instead of the reckless disregard they generally meet with. When once a road is laid out, its fate is settled, and no alteration is likely to be made: it is, therefore, the more desirable that its direction should be well studied in the first instance."

Where Should You Place Your House?

Samuel T. Maynard, *Landscape Gardening*, 1899

"Whether the house shall be on the north, south, east, or west slope is a matter of great importance in our changeable climate. On the southern, southeasterly, or southwesterly slopes a little under a hill or in the lea of a sheltering grove, the fierce northwest winds, so common throughout the country, are greatly modified, but some of our most lovely views are often lost under such conditions, and it becomes a matter of serious moment which of the two conditions to adopt. Shelter is very easily provided, however, in a short time by planting trees of rapid growth.

The location as related to the principal thoroughfare is a matter that should receive attention. On the north side of a road leading east and west, the front of the house will be open to the south, and the front rooms are thus exposed to the sun more fully than the rear rooms. If, however, more sunlight is desired in the rear rooms, a location on the south side of the street would be more satisfactory. Hallways and unoccupied rooms should be placed where there is the least sunlight.

But whatever the exposure, the aim should be to obtain shelter if possible from the prevailing winds, to secure as much sunlight as possible and preserve the most beautiful views."

Old homestead laws called for a "house twelve by fourteen" to validate a land claim. The laws didn't specify twelve feet by fourteen feet or how permanent the house had to be. Speculators found creative ways to meet the letter of the law. Be creative in placing your homestead too!

"The aspect of the dwelling should be considered in choosing a position. The fixed location of roads, rivers, or other important features in the scene, often lies in the way of a free choice in this particular. At the same time there are numberless instances in which we see great inattention to it, where there was no obstacle to its proper consideration.

The best aspect, in any country, for the principal front of a house, is that towards the fair weather quarter - that point of the compass from which the fairest and blandest wind blows most days in the year - and the worst aspect, that from which the greatest number of storms come.

Keeping these principles in view, it is evident that the south-west is the best aspect for the dwelling house in the United States, and the north-east the worst aspect. The longest, most numerous, and most disagreeable storms come from the last-named point of the compass, and the most delicious of our fair weather days are from what the Indians called the 'sweet south-west,' the land where their ideal heaven of hunting grounds lies."

Which Way Should Your New House Face?

A.J.Downing, *Hints to Young Architects*, 1847

Find an Improved Property

The American Agriculturist, August, 1862

"Any improvements already made upon a site should have considerable weight in determining one's choice. An orchard, not too old and scraggy, a few good shade trees of large size, any amount of grading, draining, manuring, fencing, etc., that may have been done, is only so much time saved, and so much money invested for the buyer's benefit. As pleasant as it is to create one's homestead wholly, yet life is short, and it is quite a help to have a few things already created to one's hand."

Does Your Land Have Character?

Samuel T. Maynard, *Landscape Gardening,* 1899

"The beauty that may be developed in any place depends largely upon the character of the land. If without character, i.e., if perfectly flat and level, no marked or strong features can be obtained except at a greatly added cost. If, however, the land is uneven, with a valley here, a hill there, a ravine in one place or a mass of bold rocks in another, much more variety and much more beautiful views may be obtained. Whatever variety is obtained on a level building lot must be made by the contrast between the ornamental trees and shrubs and the architecture."

The Perfect Site

A.J.Downing, *Hints to Persons About Building in the Country,* 1847

"It very frequently occurs that circumstances compel us to build on a particular site, so that all choice is out of the question. But as there are annually a greater number of new localities selected and built upon in this country, than in any other, the opportunity of choosing where to build is open to a large majority of those who intend erecting a country dwelling in the United States.

The best position for a dwelling house, all other things being equal, it is almost unanimously agreed, is, for an irregular country, a middle elevation, half way between the low valleys and the high hills - open to the south and west, and sheltered from the north and east."

Back in 1885, when this illustration was published in *The American Agriculturist*, moving a country building was pretty easy. You'd have a Moving-Bee, invite all your neighbors, ask them to bring their oxen, and serve refreshments. Old timber-frame buildings were strong enough to be dragged from one spot to the next.

Today, things are a bit different. With concrete foundations, hookups to septic, plumbing and heating systems and utility wires to avoid, moving a home or barn can be a very expensive proposition. I've heard that it can cost half of what the construction of the building did, and I'll bet that there isn't a contractor in the country who'll take payment in cider and doughnuts.

Most communities today have strict zoning laws that pescribe where you can build on your property. When you've determined the ideal position for your new home within those limits, have a surveyor draw it on your survey or plot plan. Then, before you build, have your contractor stake out the actual corners of the building on the ground. Measure to your property lines and check that those measurements match those on the drawing.

Don't Let This Happen to You!

Advice to Keep in View

This landscape plan, from the 1870 book, *Suburban Home Grounds*, points out a simple consideration that's often overlooked in planning or landscaping modern homes. The dotted lines projecting from the house are sight lines. By drawing them, the designer can determine which views are allowed and which are blocked by the placement of windows or by the position of trees. By drawing similar lines aimed at distant views on your plot plan or survey, you'll be able to take best advantage of them. Don't forget that the process also works in reverse. Draw sight lines from your windows to anything you'd prefer not to see, and you'll find the perfect spot for a hedge, a tree or a screen wall.

Yesterday's Site Plans

Yesterday's country homeowners took full advantage of their land. They filled their property with orchards, kitchen gardens, parklike landscapes, game fields, and countless types of outbuildings. Here are a few samples of how sites, from small to large, were planned.

Site Plans from George E. Woodward's 1867 book *Cottages and Farm Houses*

Plan for a 150'x 200' Lot

A-House; B-Stable; D-Henery; C-Manure Pit; SY-Stable Yard; H-Hot-beds; G-Dwarf Fruit-trees; N-Drying-yard; F-Raspberries, along one side of which is a Grape Arbor covering the walk; L and L-Entrances. Currants and other small fruits are planted around the outside border.

"This garden has the appearance of a much larger place than it really is; in fact, the plan could be applied to a place of ten or more acres just as well as to a limited space. The most is done to conceal the narrow limits, and leave one to guess how far one may be from the end of it when one is no more than ten feet from the well-concealed fence; at the same time, all the secondary buildings, such as barns, stables, etc., are very close to the main house, though they are entirely out of sight."

Plan for a 50'x 150' Lot

H-House; E-Entrance; O-Hot-beds; D-Dwarf fruit-trees; G-Grape trellis. The Vegetable Garden is made of four square plots.

Plan for a Five Acre Lot

A-House; B-Coach-house, Stable, Yard; C-Greenhouse and Grapery; D-Gardener's Cottage; E-Principal Entrance; F-Entrance to Barn; H-Group of Rhododendrons and Azaleas; K-Kitchen Garden; L-Entrance; N-Flower beds. In this plan the Kitchen Garden occupies about one and a half acres.

Site Design by E.Ferrand, from George E. Woodward's 1867 book *Cottages and Farm Houses*

PUB. ROAD

Plan for an Acre Lot

S-Stable and Barn; A-Greenhouse and Grapery; C-Double Henery; H-Hen Yard set with fruit-trees; D-Grape Arbor, between which and Greenhouse is a row of dwarf fruit-trees; G-Entrance; I-Dwarf and Standard fruit-trees and currants; F-Fountain; J-Flowers; O-Water-closet and Garden Tool house; E-Dwarf fruit-trees.

Site Plans from George E. Woodward's 1867 book *Cottages and Farm Houses*

Plan for a Lot of Two Acres

A-House, E-Entrance; B-Stables and Carriage House; D-Greenhouse and Grapery; I-Henery with double yard containing a few fruit-trees; SB-Strawberries; RB-Raspberries; V-Dwarf Orchard; O-Standard Orchard. Grapes are grown between the Greenhouse and Stables. The surrounding border of the Garden is set with Blackberries.

Overall View

A-the House and its Outbuildings; B-the Barnyard; C-the Orchard; D-the Kitchen Garden; E-the Fruit Garden; F-Farm Fields and Pastures; G-the Door Yard.

An American Homestead

from *The Register of Rural Affairs,* 1857

Plan

Make a Play House a Part of Your Plan

If you have kids, make sure to leave a place on your site plan for them. Find a shady, out of the way spot in your yard, and follow the old-time formula: give your children some scrap lumber, tools and nails and then leave them alone. You might want to supervise the basic structure - a frame of 2x6's nailed securely to some low tree limbs or a platform built on solid fence posts, but besides that, and checking for exposed nail points, let them build it. They'll spend countless hours planning, building and altering. They'll be exercising their bodies and their minds. In the end, they'll have something that they can truly call their own.

If their creation doesn't meet your architectural standards, it's a fault of your imagination. The illustration above is of the play house on an 1876 estate - a mansion with acres of carefully cultivated gardens whose owner hadn't forgotten his own childhood. Did you have a tree house or a quiet spot carved out of an overgrown hedge when you were young? How does that memory look today?

Advice on Home Design

Every beautiful old country home was once a a new idea in someone's imagination. To learn how some were designed so well, we can study the designers' creations and listen to their own words.

An Object for Imitation

Lewis F. Allen,
Rural Architecture, 1852

"There are found in the older states many farm and country houses that are almost models, in their way, for convenience in the main purposes required of structures of their kind, and such as can hardly be altered for the better. Yet instead of standing as objects for imitation, they have been ruled out as antiquated, and unfit for modern builders to consult, who have in the introduction of some real improvements, also left out, or discarded much that is valuable, and, where true comfort is concerned, indispensable to perfect housekeeping. In the rage for innovation of all kinds, among much that is valuable, a great deal in house-building has been introduced that is absolutely pernicious. Take, for instance, some of our ancient-looking country houses of the last century, which, in America, we call old. See their ample dimensions; their heavy, massive walls; their low, comfortable ceilings; their high gables; sharp roofs; deep porches, and spreading eaves, and contrast them with the proportionless, and card-sided things of a modern date, and draw the comparison in true comfort, which the ancient mansion really affords, by the side of the other."

Calvert Vaux,
Villas & Cottages, 1867

"All previous experience in architecture is the inherited property of America, and should be taken every advantage of. Each beautiful thought, form, and mode that is not unsuited to the climate and the people, ought to be studied, sifted, and tested, its principles elucidated, and itself improved, on."

"Those who have watched the progress of Rural Architecture for some years past, have noticed a marked advance in architectural design and proportion and convenient and economical interior arrangement; yet, compared with the large number of structures yearly put up, the really attractive and tasteful buildings form the exception, and not the rule. Building, at best, is an expensive undertaking, and those who engage in it without availing themselves of the progressive improvements of the day, make investments from which it is difficult to realize first cost; while he who embraces the principles of beauty, harmony, good taste, etc., rarely fails to command his customer, and a handsome profit when ready to sell. The fact we desire to impress most thoroughly is, that it costs no more to build correctly and beautifully than to ignore all rules of taste, and that every one in this broad land who means to have a home of his own, should have a home worth owning."

Good Design is Your Best Investment

George E. Woodward, *Cottages & Farm Houses*, 1867

How to Choose Your Home's Style

The Register of Rural Affairs, 1865

"To harmonize with the surrounding scenery, to enter into the spirit of the landscape, is the highest beauty of a domestic building. This is too often overlooked;—and we find the dignity and repose of Nature broken by the presence of white, bare, bleak abodes, set ostentatiously in unplanted fields. Flat roofs and horizontal lines are opposed to the ascending lines of rocks and mountains around them; lofty turrets and steep gables rise up to contradict the natural expression of level plains. A house may be considered beautiful in the situation which suits it; its precise copy, in an unfit place, will always be a miserable deformity."

A.J.Downing, *Hints to Young Architects*, 1847

"The simplest rule for determining what style of building is best adapted to a particular kind of scenery, is to determine first the character of both the architecture and the landscape in question. Our own maxim is, that the bolder and more irregular the scenery, the bolder and more irregular the style of architecture it demands. Hence, building with highly varied outlines, with towers and the like, are most fittingly placed amid bold hills, and in a broken and mountainous country.

For a flat or level country, almost any simple style of building is in good keeping, Hence the propriety of the modifications of the cottage and villa forms which generally prevail there, and which are always pleasing when they express the simple life of the country gentleman, farmer, or proprietor of the soil—and equally unpleasing when they exhibit the finery of town houses, or ambitious architectural ornaments not properly answering to the habits or wants of their inhabitants."

Lewis F. Allen, *Rural Architecture*, 1852

"The site selected for the dwelling, and the character of the scenery and objects immediately surrounding it, should have a controlling influence upon the style in which the house is to be constructed. A fitness and harmony in all these is indispensable."

"*Fashion is not the synonym of taste; nor is beauty monopolized by wealth. A low log-cabin, nestled in the woods, the moss grown over its roof, the morning-glories climbing to the rustic window, is more attractive and is a better home than many a costly marble mansion. But the effort of 'putting the best foot foremost,' and anxiously attempting much display, costs our country homes the truth, the comfort, the sobriety which ought to characterize their architecture.*

No house can fail to please whose form and hue accord with the adjacent country; which looks just what it is, neither less nor more; whose proportions and details are formed upon the principles of taste; and whose inner arrangement regards economy of space and gives attention to the laws of health, - requiring the fewest steps, presenting the greatest cheerfulness, neatness and convenience for common and daily use. All which the poorest man who builds can have as well as the rich; for Providence opens a short road to comfort, but hedges up the path to luxury."

Common Sense Design is Always in Fashion

The Register of Rural Affairs,
1865

"*Proportion may be shown in the smallest cottage as well as in the most magnificent palace - and the former should be carefully designed as well as the latter.*"

The Register of Rural Affairs,
1856

Country Style & Materials

Lewis F. Allen,
Rural Architecture, 1852

"As a general remark, all buildings should show for themselves, what they are built of. Let stone be stone; bricks show on their own account; and of all things, put no counterfeit by way of plaster, stucco, or other false pretense other than paint, or a durable wash upon wood: it is a miserable affectation always, and of no possible use whatever."

Henry W. Cleaveland, *Village & Farm Cottages*, 1856

"When we are considering a structure, as a whole, or in its parts, with reference to appearance and expression, rather than mere utility and comfort, a close adherence to right principles of design is peculiarly desirable. Although this will set aside many fanciful forms which are common and fashionable, there is no danger of its producing an unpleasing uniformity. While the surface and scenery of the country exhibit an unbounded diversity, and the condition, character, and tastes of our countrymen are almost as various, our architecture, if properly conformed to these, incurs no danger of tiring by its sameness."

The Value of Simple Design

Calvert Vaux,
Villas & Cottages, 1867

"It is difficult to perceive, amid the glitter of ornament, the superior dignity and beauty of simplicity. We confess as hearty a love of decoration and ornament in architecture as any one. But it must be consistent, to satisfy us. It must express a beauty which pervades the building itself, everywhere, and not seem patched on, to catch the eye, and hide its defects. Harmonious proportions, a well ordered distribution of parts, excellent constructions, and afterwards, a suitable degree of decorations. Else it is like a poor book badly printed, yet richly bound and glittering with gold leaf.

A simple, well-planned structure costs less to execute, for the accommodation obtained, than an ill-planned one; and the fact of its being agreeable and effective, or otherwise, does not depend on any ornament that may be superadded to the useful and necessary forms of which it is composed, but on the arrangement of those forms themselves, so that they may balance each other and suggest the pleasant ideas of harmonious proportion, fitness, and agreeable variety to the eye, and through the eye to the mind. All this is simply a matter of study before building, not of additional cost in building."

What Shape Should Your New House Be ?

A.J.Downing, *Hints to Young Architects*, 1847

"All builders will agree that the most economical form in which a dwelling can be erected is a cube, because it contains more space within a given area of walls and roof than any other. Next to this is a parallelogram. The more irregular the outline of a building, the more the cost is increased, because it has more exterior surface, and therefore requires more wall or weather boarding, more roof, more gutters, and more fixtures and ornaments, when the house is in a handsome style.

On the other hand, the irregular form has great advantages, not only in the greater beauty of effect which the architect is enabled to bestow on it, but in its variety of sizes, forms, and consequently accommodation of its apartments within, as well as in the greater number and variety of views afforded without.

Hence, those who desire to combine as much economy as possible, with good taste in building a residence, will select a cube or rectangle for the outline of its ground plan; while those to whom expense is of less importance than convenience and picturesque effect, will adopt the irregular form.'"

"It will be apparent, without special argument, that our choice of style in our country houses should be controlled essentially by the climate. In northern climate, the flat roof is objectionable. The hot summer sun will be more than likely to open the joints and seams of the flat roof, and the sudden shower coming down with the force of a tropical storm, will find its way through, sadly to the detriment of our ceilings, our stuccoes and frescoes, as well as to the comfort and the commendable equability of temper of those who suffer the invasion. The heavy winter snows, too, require a steep roof, from which they will readily dislodge themselves without Injury.

And so in the interior arrangements of the house the provisions for heating and ventilation, for summer freedom and winter coziness, for domestic comfort and the exercise of the commendable grace of country hospitality, due regard must be had to the conditions of climate. There must be a proper adaptation to them, if we would secure satisfactory country homes."

Build for Your Climate

George E. Woodward, *Cottages & Farm Houses*, 1867

An 1884 Connecticut farmstead by architect S.B.Reed

A New England Farmstead

Cold, snowy, windy New England winters made farmers' hard work even harder. In the worst of weather, outdoor work was impossible, and even the walk to the dairy barn was a dangerous adventure.

Yankee ingenuity created a solution. By connecting their buildings, one to another, farmers could walk under cover to their chores. Woodsheds, wagon houses and workshops became a link between farmhouses and barns. The connected buildings faced south, with most of the windows and doors on that side. The buildings created a wall to the north winds that made a warm work yard just outside the front doors.

If you're building in a cold climate, wall off the winter with the layout of your home and garage.

A Southern Home

Any home built in a warm climate or for use as a summer house should be designed to keep itself cool. This 1876 cottage, by architect Isaac H. Hobbs, shows some of the best methods. Porches, window hoods and deep roof overhangs provide shade and allow the windows to remain open in a cooling rain. The kitchen, where most heat is generated, is separate from the main body of the house. Warm air from it, and from all of the other rooms in the house, can be vented through the upper level windows of the entry hall.

First Floor Plan

Some Home Design Hints

The Register of Rural Affairs, 1858

"However small a building may be, let it never show an awkward conception, when a good form is more easily made than a bad one."

"A profusion of decoration, or 'gingerbread work,' so often seen, more commonly shows a want of true architectural taste than its presence."

"In all cases study beauty of form and proportion, and not ornament. Tasteful simplicity is better than fanciful complexity -as a statue in simple drapery is better than one bedizzened with feathers, ribbons, and unmeaning gewgaws."

A.J. Downing, *The Horticulturist,* 1848

"Do not attempt to build a dwelling upon your farm after the fashion of the town-house of your friend, the city merchant; do not attempt to give the modest little cottage the ambitious air of the ornate villa. Be assured that there is, if you will search for it, a peculiar beauty to each of these classes of dwellings that heightens and adorns it almost magically; while if it borrows the ornaments of the other, it is only debased and falsified in character and expression."

When 19th century architect Andrew Jackson Downing designed his own country home, shown above, he spared no expense. He built in the latest fashion, with elaborate shapes and details and the most expensive materials. He impressed his friends and clients but drove his family to debt and poverty that eventually led to the loss of the place.

How much better would one of his simple cottage designs have been? His 1850, "Bracketed Cottage," shown below would have been a fraction of the cost. It's a more elegant design in its simplicity.

Every extra that you put into your new place means extra construction cost, and extra cost every year, forever, in maintenance and taxes. Country views, fresh air and foliage are luxuries that you'll enjoy more from the front porch of a comfortable cabin than you will from the verandah of a villa that you have to worry about affording.

Plan on a Design That You Can Afford

Don't Build Too Tall

The illustration above, from the 1900 book, *The Farmstead,* was drawn to illustrate a common mistake in country building design. A home, barn or outbuilding that's too tall always looks awkward in the countryside, particularly when set in an open, treeless field. Study the prettiest country places that you know, and you'll see that they tend to spread wide and hug the land.

One-floor porches and extending ells, and low outbuildings, surrounding a two or three floor house will improve the appearance of your country place. Low extensions will weave your design into the landscape and make your place seem like it belongs on its land.

Avoid Stylish Homes

The farm cottage shown on the next page was the height of fashion when it was built. By the time the illustration was drawn, it was hopelessly out of date. Today we view Gothic style homes as quaint curiosities. Interesting and fun to look at, but not what we'd want to live in.

The great thing about building in the country is that the countryside is its own decoration. You don't have to be stylish to have a beautiful home. Build a plain place with good proportions and simple materials and let nature do the rest. Nature is always in style, with the perfect new look every season.

"A small farm house on a modest-sized farm is shown above. The site is beautiful, and is worthy of a house better fitted to the situation, the farm, and the farmer. The illustration shows seven gables, and the house, therefore, might serve as a model for a work of fiction; but the left-hand side of the house is like unto the right-hand side, so it will not do for fiction, for if the truth must be told, there are eleven gables and twenty-two valleys on this house.

The vine-covered veranda is most beautiful, and looks cool and comfortable, but there are too many vines, and, with the exception of a few days in summer at midday, the air under this veranda would be damp and uncomfortable. It is far better to secure shade by means of awnings and a few tall, well trimmed shade trees, which preclude dampness and permit air drainage. than to overburden the veranda with vines. The covering off this veranda is an unprotected floor, and extends along the front and well around both sides. Notice the too expensive balustrade and frequent fancy posts, an enlarged section of which is shown. All of this expensive wooden material is exposed to our ever-changeful, paint-destroying climate. The tinsmith, the painter, and the carpenter will reap a rich harvest if the external part of this house is kept in order."

Don't Over-Do Your Design

Isaac Phillips Roberts, *The Farmstead*, 1900

Uncommon Shapes are a Common Mistake

Yesterday's designers experimented with unusual shapes for their structures. Octagonal houses and round barns were, briefly, quite popular. The reason you don't see too many of those buildings today is that the experiments were failures. The added expense of construction and awkward interior spaces that resulted made builders appreciate the advantage of square and rectangular plans.

The design of your new country home is too important to be either a fad or an experiment. Traditional design solutions became the tradition because they worked. Build a square-cornered country home - it will cost you less and it will fit your furniture.

"In its main characteristics this house resembles the Swiss cottage. Circumstances similar to those which make this style proper on the Alpine slopes often exist among us, and it is for some such position that the design is intended. It would suit well the southern side of some steep and rugged hill, and will look all the better if the grounds around and below it are left with their natural inequalities, and not tortured into terraces or graded into tameness."

Use a World of Ideas

Henry W. Cleaveland, *Village & Farm Cottages*, 1856

19th Century architects searched the world for building ideas. Any style was appropriate as long as it suited its terrain. You have the same options. Study the vernacular architecture of places that match your site's climate. And don't limit yourself to buildings in exotic locations. The vernacular designs that worked well for hundreds of years in the area where you're building should be your first source of inspiration.

Be a Pioneer

By 1889, when this "Cabin in Texas" was published in the book *Log Cabins and Cottages: How to Build and Furnish Them*, log houses were rarely built of necessity. At the turn of the 20th century ,it was more common for logs to be used to build an Adirondack summer home for a wealthy New York family than for a true settlement cabin. Log building had become a fad that was used because the style evoked images of America's pioneer spirit.

The first log homes, the true pioneer cabins, were marvels of efficiency. The same trees that had to be cleared off the land to create farm fields were simply stacked to form walls. Later, as the farm prospered, these walls were simply sheathed in clapboard as the cabin became a wing of a larger, more elegant home.

Today, pioneering buildings come in all shapes, materials and styles. Modern engineering is improving modular buildings, panelized construction and even log-home kits. Artisans are rediscovering the advantages of old construction methods like timber-framing and adobe and applying them to modern home building. A well designed and engineered home, built to modern standards and code requirements, will be more durable, healthier, more energy efficient and safer than anything built in the past. Read books like this one to find old-time design ideas for the layout, details and appearance of your new home, but don't ignore new ideas too.

Calvert Vaux,
Villas & Cottages,
1867

" The past should always be looked on as a servant, not as a master."

There are quite a few advantages to building a home into the side of a hill. The natural flow of rain water downhill and breezes uphill will keep it cooler and dryer. Simply adding large windows to the half exposed foundation walls will make bright and airy living space where a basement would have been. Rooms on the lower level, protected by the earth of the hill, will be warmer in winter and cooler in summer.

Consider a Hillside House

Convert an Old Building

If your country property has an old building on it, consider a creative renovation. Because they tend to have large open spaces, old barns, carriage houses and garages are fairly easy to convert into homes. You'll save some cost and save a bit of our heritage.

This cottage, from the 1856 book, *Village & Farm Cottages,* was converted from an old coach-house. The 20 x 20' floor area is just about the same as a modern two-car garage. The owner built a new steep roof to provide a second floor with usable space, then added the partitions, windows, doors and verandah that you see. The term, "Living Room," in the 19th century, simply meant the room in which the family members spent most of their time. In this design, it's a combination kitchen and dining room.

Lower Level Plan

Phase 2

Phase 3

Phase 1

The Finished House

It was common practice in the past to build small and add rooms as needed. This design, from George Woodward's 1867 book, *Architecture and Rural Art*, shows how it should be done. The finished house was envisioned from the start. The second floor, staircase, chimney and entry door were built first to remain through all the changes. New rooms were built on the outside of the old structure, and passage doors replaced windows. With careful planning of the new construction, family life was disturbed as little as possible.

"Build a permanent home - or the beginning of one - at the outset. Build the home now, and though you commence with only a kitchen and a bedroom, the seasons will come and go, bringing their gifts of improvement and beauty, and thirty years hence your home will be a far sweeter and lovelier abode than any grand new house, at such a time, can possibly be."

Plan on a Home that Grows with Your Needs

E.H.Leland, *Farm Homes,* 1882

Design a Place That's on the Square

Yesterday's builders and today's will tell you the importance of building plumb, square and level from the start. Minor wobbles in the foundation and first plates and sills tend to grow into major problems as a building rises higher. Out-of-kilter walls make installing cabinets, tile, doors, windows and even wallpaper much more difficult. A little time spent with a square and a level, early in the building process, will repay itself again and again, over the years.

But, there's an even more important way that yesterday's country builders stayed "on-the-square." One of the most unappreciated features of picture-perfect farmsteads and country villages is that most nearby buildings have their walls parallel to each other. Old farm barns and outbuildings are almost always square with the farmhouse. Extensions and ells of buildings continue in the same direction as the main roof ridge or turn at a right, ninety degree, or "square" angle. The buildings all have walls that face the street, or the points of the compass, straight on.

In villages, the same is true from house to house and from shop to shop. Homes were built at the same distance back from the road. That was considered neighborly. Old-time good manners seemed to be more effective than today's zoning laws in maintaining good setbacks.

We see old country buildings as parts of a composition and not as individual pieces. Their square orderliness joins one to another, so the beauty of the best structures spreads to improve the look of lesser buildings. The orderliness also presents the buildings in wonderful contrast to the chaos of nature and the flowing patchwork quilt of farm fields.

If you're constructing a home with a garage, a barn or a stable, or even just a shed, plan your buildings so that they are on-the-square with each other. Be gracious and keep the same angles and setbacks that your neighbors' buildings have. You'll be keeping up a great tradition, and your place and your neighborhood will look much better for the trouble.

Planning Your Rooms

You'll need to carefully plan the number, size and type of rooms in the design
of your country home. Here is some advice that should help.

Plan on Using The Outdoors

The first space to think about when you plan your country home is the outdoors. Why live in the country if you're not planning to enjoy your property? Plan on porches, decks, arbors and patios that extend your new home to the outdoors.

A kitchen porch was a common feature on old farmhouses. Build one as an inexpensive, outdoor kitchenette. Add a sleeping porch or balcony to a bedroom. Plan a breezeway between your home and garage as an outdoor family room.

There's one way that yesterday's buildings had an advantage in using the land. Without modern earth-moving equipment to level hills, builders had to carefully carve foundations into the sides of hills. That gave level access to the ground at two or more floors of homes, barns and backbuildings. If you have a hillside site, use it to your advantage. Have a quiet shady patio off of an upstairs bedroom or a basement playroom that opens to the yard. You home will look more at one with its site, you'll do less damage to your land, and you'll get more enjoyment of the nicest space you have.

"1. Let the kitchen (the most important apartment) always be on a level with the principal floor—and for strong light and free ventilation, it should have, if possible, windows on opposite or nearly opposite sides.

2. The pantry or dish-closet should be between the kitchen and dining-room, and easily accessible from both.

3. There should be a set of easy stairs from the kitchen to the cellar, and also an outer set into the cellar for admitting barrels, etc.

4. More attention should be given to the arrangement and convenient disposition of such rooms as are in constant use, than those but occasionally occupied. Hence the kitchen and living room should receive more attention on the ground of convenience, than the parlor.

5. Every entrance, except to the kitchen, should be through some entry or hall, to prevent the abrupt ingress of cold air, and for proper seclusion.

6. Let the entry or hall be near the center of the house, so that ready and convenient access may be had from it to the different rooms; and to prevent the too common evil of passing through one room to enter another.

7. Place the stairs so that the landing shall be as near the center as may be practicable, for the reason given for the preceding rule.

8. Let the partitions of the second floor stand over those of the lower, as nearly as may be, to secure firmness and solidity."

Advice on Planning Your Country Home

The Register of Rural Affairs, 1857

The Entry

E.H.Leland, *Farm Homes,*
1882

"If one's house must be small and the rooms few, still a hall or some sort of pleasant vestibule ought to be afforded, rather than have the living-room or parlor open abruptly into the open air. It is good for family habits, too, that the children have a regular place for hats and caps, and an opportunity before a hall mirror to see that they are presentable prior to appearing in the sitting or dining-room. Such little household regulations teach children order and self-control.

This moral view of the Hall brings up another consideration. There are many kind-hearted, fair-minded house-keepers who regard the main entrance of their houses as being too sacred for daily use, and prefer that husband and children and intimate friends should "run around" to a side or a kitchen door. This is a mistake. Better live in a hut with but one entrance than have a door-way too grand for those nearest us to walk through!

But these same fair-minded house-keepers will exclaim, 'Oh, it is all very well to talk about the footsteps of those nearest us, but I can't afford to have my hall-carpet covered with mud every day and torn to tatters in six months!'

Of course you cannot afford it, nor can you afford to have your children acquire the careless manners and habits that come of the back-door principle. Have a door-mat at the hall door, and teach little feet to respect it."

Avoid North Entrances

"A due north aspect is a very objectionable one for a country house, not only on account of the bad weather to which it exposes the principal side of the house, but also because of the accumulation of snow and ice about it in winter, rendering it far more difficult to keep it in hospitable order than a house with a warm southern entrance front.

For a country house which is only intended for summer use, the owner of which leaves it for town in winter, this is not a valid objection. Indeed, a northern entrance is, in our mid-summer, more agreeable, perhaps, than a southern one - its piazzas always cool, and its view opening upon the best and brightest face of the lawn and trees - that turned towards the sun. But the comparatively short season to which this can, in our latitude, be applied with truth, renders a northern aspect a very objectionable one for families residing in the country during the whole year."

A.J.Downing, *Hints to Young Architects*, 1847

Attic Bedrooms

Calvert Vaux, *Villas & Cottages,*
1867

"Attic bedrooms may be so planned as to afford a valuable addition to the accommodation of a country house. A more extended view is generally to be obtained from these rooms than from the rest of the house, and as they may be made quite as comfortable, though not, of course, so symmetrical, as the second floor chambers, they deserve a fair share of consideration; and the economical advantages they offer have frequently led me, in practice, to advise the use of a high-pitched roof. The acute angle of the roof precludes the possibility of any large surface being exposed to the vertical rays of the sun, and the flat on the top, being furred down some three or four feet, supplies an air-chamber above the attic ceiling that acts as a satisfactory shield from the heat."

"*The windows and Venetian blinds are tightly closed, the door is tightly shut, and the best room, that I am now thinking of, is, in consequence, always ready for - what? for daily use? Oh, no; it is in every way too good for that. For weekly use? No, not even for that - but for company use; and thus the choice room with the pretty view, is sacrificed, to keep up a conventional show of finery that pleases no one, and is a great, though unacknowledged, bore to the proprietors. Such is one style of best parlor to be found in America; and though it is by no means universal, it is far too general for comfort. A drawing room like this becomes a sort of quarantine in which to put each plague of a visitor that calls; and one almost expects to see the lady of the house walk in with a bottle of camphor in her hand, to prevent infection, she seems to have such a fear that any one should step within the bounds of her real every-day home life. All this is absurd. No room in any house, except, perhaps, in a very large mansion, ought to be set apart for company use only. If a reception-room for strangers is needed, it should be a small, unpretending room, certainly not the most agreeably situated apartment in the house, which should be enjoyed daily, for it is not the having any good thing, but the using it, that gives it its value.*"

Do You Need a Parlor ?

Calvert Vaux, *Villas & Cottages,* 1867

Bad Manners: 1-Tips back his chair; 2-Eats with his mouth too full; 3-Feeds a dog at the table; 4-Holds his knife improperly; 5-Engages in a violent argument at the meal-time; 6-Lounges upon the table; 7-Brings a cross child to the table; 8-Drinks from the saucer and laps with his toung to the last drop from the plate; 9-Comes to the table with his shirt-sleeves and puts his feet beside his chair; 10-Picks his teeth with his fingers; 11-Scratches her head and is frequently unnecessarily getting up from the table.

Illustrations from *Hill's Manual of Social and Business Forms*, 1886, "Gentility in the Dining Room," opposite and "Bad Manners at the Table," above.

"*There is nothing more essential to the comfort, and consequently to the happiness, of the family, than that the dining-room should be, of all the apartments of the house, the most pleasant and the most attractive. And, to this end, the first requisite is, that it should be properly placed. In building, or in the occupation of the residence already constructed, let that room be selected for the purpose into which the morning sun at least shall throw its cheerful rays. In a cold climate, at no time is its presence more welcome than at the breakfast-table. If practicable, let both the morning and evening sunlight illuminate the room. These points can be attained by the choice of the southeastern exposure.*"

The Dining Room

George E. Woodward, *Cottages and Farm Houses*, 1867

Plan on an Extra First Floor Room

It's rare to find a country home plan published in an old farm journal that doesn't have a "chamber" shown on the main floor. Folk lore says that a first floor bedroom was a "birthing room," and it was. But, it was also a children's play room, a sick room, a bedroom for extra farm hands at harvest time, Grandma's room, a guest room and whatever else it was needed to be for ever-changing country life.

Within the scope of building a new country home, one additional room isn't too expensive, and it might make all the difference in how useful and enjoyable your new place is after it's new. Use it now as an entertainment room or home office, tomorrow as a nursery, later as family den and later still as a place where your grandchildren stay when they visit. Someday you'll tire of taking the stairs and be glad for the option of a bedroom on the first floor.

"Kitchens should be too small for setting a table, and if there is any probability of undertaking such a thing, they should be still smaller. If there is any one thing better calculated than another to weaken digestion, mar the pleasure of eating, grate upon delicate nerves, and harrow up the feelings generally of persons of some degree of culture and refinement, it is to sit down to meals in a room impregnated with the odors of cooking, with stove close at hand containing steaming pots and boilers of turnip, cabbage or potato water, and the greasy liquid in which meat or fish was cooked; on the other side perhaps a shelf or sink, containing the endless list that will accumulate in cooking, of dirty dishes, pans, spiders, skillets, griddle greasers, and what not, that in the hurry to have the meal at the exact minute, must be tossed into the nearest catch-all. Oh, what a place for that social and intellectual feast - that warm commingling of the feelings and affections which in some families can occur only at meal time, as then only will all the members be together - even family worship will probably be conducted here! Is this picture too strong? 'You don't have things so.' Perhaps not. But others must admit, at least to themselves, that it may be even worse."

The Advantage of a Small Kitchen

The Register of Rural Affairs,
1873

"A Virginia Cabin," from the 1899 book, *Log Cabins and Cottages: How to Build and Furnish Them*

Have a Dog-Trot to Cool Your Home

Pioneer log building has its limitations. The length that any wall could be was limited by the height of straight tree trunks on the land and the weight of a log that one or two people could lift. It's rare for an old log building to have any walls that are longer than sixteen feet.

When a barn or cabin needed to be larger than sixteen feet by sixteen feet, pioneers built a series of small rooms and joined them under the same roof. One of the most common arrangements was the "Dog-trot." It was two log rooms, really two separate cabins, connected by a roof. The space between them was an open porch.

This type of cabin became popular throughout the south. Dogs and their masters found that the open bay, between two long flat walls, acted as a funnel for cooling breezes. The exact same configuration, a covered, open space between a home and a barn or garage, is the common "breezeway" of New England and Midwest country homes.

If you're building in the South, or want a cool outdoor space in summer, build a Dog-trot.

Country Details

After you've determined your new home's location on your property, its orientation, the general style and shape, and the number and type of rooms you need, it's time to start thinking about details. Here are some ideas for your consideration.

Have a Country Fireplace

George E. Woodward, *Cottages and Farm Houses*, 1867

"What we consider indispensable in a country house, be it large or small, is an old fashioned open fire-place, for burning wood on the hearth, if wood can be had, or, if not, coal in the grate, and, besides, for purposes of ventilation. We think, for practical reasons, the old poetic sentiment of the family fireside and the blazing log should not be lost sight of, and there should be at least one room in every house - the room that is the most used by the family as a sitting-room - made attractive and healthy by this means."

E.H. Leland, *Farm Homes*, 1882

"A fire-place goes farther than anything else in giving to a room character and beauty. In the cool weather of spring and fall, when the morning and evening air is a little sharp, or when a long cold rainstorm is making everything damp, moist and uncomfortable, there is nothing more delightful than a brisk fire on an open hearth."

"The upper horizontal line of the span roof, with its handsome gables, will generally afford the beholder most pleasure, and appears to harmonize best with country scenery. There is also a practical reason for it worth considering. The good housewife prizes a fine, open garret for many purposes. Not the least of these is having a place for drying clothes in cold or stormy weather, where they can hang regardless of thieves or sudden rain, until she is ready to iron them. This is a principal reason why at least one wing of some of the other designs is carried up two stories when good proportion in so narrow a building seems to require less height. The roofs also are pretty steep, allowing snow and rain to slip off easily, making the roof more durable, beside giving better head room.

This also is rather in violation of what is usually taught in architectural works, for there we are apt to find the flattest roofs on two-story houses. The idea appears to be that the house with steep roof, being actually higher, must necessarily appear so. This I believe to be a mistake, at least on rather narrow buildings. Having given particular attention to the subject for some time past, and made many comparisons, it is found that houses with flattish roofs invariably look higher than their steeper roofed neighbors. It would appear that we judge mainly by apparent height of the sides, or distance from side eaves to the ground."

A Country House Needs a Gable Roof

The Register of Rural Affairs, 1874

Donald G. Mitchell, *Rural Studies,*
1867

A Country Home Needs a Porch

"A country house without a porch is like a man without an eyebrow; it gives expression, and gives expression where you most want it. The least office of a porch is that of affording protection against the rain-beat and sun-beat. It is an interpreter of character; it humanizes bald walls and windows; it emphasizes architectural tone; it gives hint of hospitality; it is a hand stretched out (figuratively and lumberingly, often) from the world within to the world without."

E.H. Leland, *Farm Homes,* 1882

"Verandas are most desirable on the south and west sides of a house, for while they ward off the mid-day heat of summer, they still freely admit the low down winter sun."

"The veranda is perhaps the most specially American feature in a country house; nothing can compensate for its absence, and endless opportunities for variety in design occur in treating this part of a country house."

Calvert Vaux, *Villas & Cottages,* 1867

"To build a substantial roof with a veranda round the whole cottage, or round three sides of it, would be too expensive an outlay for most occupants of such a dwelling. This arbor, which is barely the skeleton of such a veranda - being, in fact, only an arbor with rather better posts than usual, would cost but little, and would not only be productive of much beauty, but a good deal of profit. We suppose it to be covered with those two best and hardiest of our native grapes - the Isabella and Catawba - the most luxuriant growers in all soils - affording the finest shade, and, in the middle and western States, giving large and regular crops of excellent fruit."

An Arbor Veranda

A.J.Downing, *The Architecture of Country Homes,* 1852

A High Porch

Are you building a home at the seaside or in rolling country? There is probably a view that would be much more dramatic from the second floor. This 1867 cottage design, by architect George E. Harney, shows one way of taking advantage of the vista. By building the roof of the entry porch higher and using the space created as an open balcony, the architect captured views and cool night breezes. In winter, storm windows change the space into a "conservatory," a sunny, protected spot for potted plants that wouldn't survive the cold.

Welcome Your Guests

Gracious entry portals were as important to yesterday's home builders as they should be to today's. Page through this book, and you'll see dozens of ways to make your main entrance attractive and inviting, from simple shed-roof door hoods to elegant colonnades. Here are a couple of ideas that seem just right for country homes - rose covered columns from an 1880's farm journal and comfortable, useful front-door benches from the 1852 book *The Architecture of Country Houses,* by Andrew Jackson Downing.

Closets

Francis C. Moore, *How to Build a Home*, 1897

The American Agriculturist, 1874

"Closets are indispensable for comfort, and should be numerous. It is safe to assume that it is wise to sacrifice floor-space of rooms for closets, for they secure not only comfort, but order and neatness in the appearance of the house. The specifications should name the height and width of shelves, distance between them, size and arrangement of drawers, and should require hooks for hanging, which will cost little more if of brass or bronze instead of iron, and should be double. The door should not swing into a closet, thus doing away with half the hanging room, to say nothing of injury to the contents; and yet this is a common fault with some architects and builders. Examine the plans to see that the hooks in closets for hanging clothing are at the proper height from the floor, and that the shelves above the hooks start at a sufficient height above them to give room for removing garments. Any practical housekeeper will say that the house cannot have too many closets."

"Having suffered some for closet room at one time or another, or for places to stow away things, I have had considerable sympathy with the man who said that when he built a house he should begin with a big closet and make additions to that."

Doors

A.W. Brunner, *Cottages or Hints on Economical Building,* 1884

"Doors are generally hung according to the sweet will of the carpenter, but there are two ways to hand a door, one so as to expose the room, the other so as to screen it. The first may be good for the more public rooms, but, in regard to bed-rooms, the doors must swing so that, when partly open, they will shield the apartment from view. Closet doors should be hung so that the closet may receive light from the nearest window. Doors are sometimes made to swing out on stair landings or halls, and who has not seen two doors so placed that they strike each other when opened? It is hardly necessary to say that these methods should not be adopted."

Country Windows

Last century's homes had more window area than today's do. That's logical for a time when rooms were lit only by candles or the sun. A formula that was often repeated in yesterday's building guides calls for one square inch of window area for every cubic foot of room volume. In a 12' x 16' bed room with an 8' high ceiling, that means three 2' wide by 4' high windows, or a third more than most modern builders would use.

The old formula seems just right for a new country home. If you're building in the country for the clean air, cool breezes and pretty views, you should keep it in mind.

"Where economy is necessary, doors and windows should be what are called 'stock' sizes, i.e., the regular sizes made by the mills of the vicinity in which the dwelling is to be located. To specify them will save the expense inseparable from unusual or irregular sizes. If, however, the house is so located as to have a fine view, it will be mistaken economy not to have one or more of the prominent windows wider."

Francis C. Moore, *How to Build a Home*, 1897

Exterior Details

Calvert Vaux, *Villas & Cottages*, 1867

"The bay-window is the peculiar feature next to the verandah that an American rural home loves to indulge in. There can, indeed, scarcely be too many for the comfort of the house, or too few for the comfort of the purse, for I regret to add that they are expensive features. The simplest form is a plain semi-octagon, with simple shed-roof, shown above. This sort of bay is very commonly finished with a roof running up to a point against the wall; but the effect thus produced is always mean and disagreeable, and a straight line for some distance, as shown on the sketch, gives the appearance of the windows belonging to the house much more than the other mode.

The balcony is a feature that can now and then be introduced to advantage; and a specimen that tells the whole story, and scarcely needs any further detail, is shown in the illustration.

Dormer-windows are of several sorts, according to the style of the house. They are often made too small, and considerable comfort and effect is thereby lost, for a small one costs very nearly as much as a large one, and is not half so available. A dormer is a capital feature in a country house."

"If bay windows are too expensive, a very desirable substitute can be had by placing two ordinary sized windows side by side with a wide capacious ledge at the bottom for seats or for plants.

A room with a window like this cannot fail to be cheery, and its effect in a simple cottage house is quite sumptuous. There is likewise in its favor the fact that it is less exposed than the deep bay window to outer heat and cold.

In a kitchen or in a child's bedroom, or in an attic where the walls are low, two half-windows set side by side and made to slide or to open on hinges, admit a broad, generous light, and give an apartment a pretty and pleasing rustic air.

In the country, with a whole sky to draw from, let there be light! If any rooms in the house must look solely to the north for illumination, let them be the parlor and the spare chamber. People who come and go can be cheerful for a while in a north-windowed apartment, but the constant dwellers in a house need its sunniest rooms."

A Substitute for Bay Windows

E.H.Leland, *Farm Homes,* 1882

Details that Keep a House Dry

This cottage, from the 1850 book, *The Architecture of Country Houses*, is a model of how a house can be designed to keep itself dry. The simple, sloping roof projects broadly to carry rain and snow away from the walls. The hoods over the windows and door protect them, even when they are left open. The horizontal band of wood, just above the foundation, is a "water-table." It is beveled away from the house to carry off any water that runs down the walls. As you can see, the first floor is built two steps above the ground which is also terraced around the house. Water would have to climb uphill to get in.

Illustration of a door hood, from the 1867 book, *Villas & Cottages*

Window Hoods

Calvert Vaux, *Villas & Cottages*, 1867

"Hoods to windows in American country houses are features that seem to spring naturally from the peculiarities of the climate, and the needs they give rise to. The upper sashes of windows with hoods can always be left a little open without any chance of the rain beating in; and even when of small size they protect the glass from the direct vertical rays of the summer sun, and receive the first blows from the winter storm. They also add much to the artistic effect of a rural building.

It is to be observed that, in summer, a small window is in one respect most comfortable, as a wall is a better protection from heat than glass or Venetian blinds. But, on the other hand, large windows are desirable to throw open for the summer evening breeze, and to let in plenty of cheerful light during dull winter and spring days. The hood, in a measure, connects these two opposite needs. A veranda all round a house is delightful for a month or two in the heat of summer; but most healthily-constituted persons like to have the opportunity to admit a stream of glorious, warm, genial sunlight into their rooms whenever they feel inclined to enjoy it, and this can not be obtained if the veranda entirely encircles the living apartments. The hood, on the other hand, defends the window from the powerful rays of the mid-day sun without shutting it out entirely."

Illustration of a window hood and stone water-table, from *Villas & Cottages*

The Advantage of a Steep Roof

Yesterday's country home builders knew the advantages of steep roofs. Since they shed water and snow more quickly, they lasted longer.

The real advantage though, is the space that a steep roof creates. The Cross Section of a house, from the 1856 book, *Village & Farm Cottages*, shows that although the entire second floor is below the line of the roof, it's still completely habitable.

An attic room is a very inexpensive space. You have to build the roof structure and gable walls anyway. All you need are extra windows, interior finishes, heat or air conditioning and electricity. If you're building on a budget, consider planning some rooms below a steep roof.

Section

"The additions of porches, verandas, bay-windows, etc., increase the effect of cottage-houses to a very considerable degree, add much to interior convenience and beauty, and, if put on at the time when the building is constructed, do not materially augment the expense. We think they are always worth their full cost, and rarely fail to make an impression upon the eye of a purchaser.

The place designed simply for a summer residence for the citizen, who is obliged to be at his office or counting room daily, barring the few weeks of summer vacation, need not be so complete in its appointments and arrangements, as the permanent country residence. One essential condition, however, in this case is, that there shall be room enough, with ample verandahs, and shaded gravel walks, which will afford opportunities for open air exercise in all states of the weather. There is nothing, perhaps, that interferes so essentially with the citizen's enjoyment of the country, as the want of facilities for out door exercise. It is too hot or too dusty to ride or walk, before the shower, and after its refreshment has come, it is wet and muddy. Build spacious verandahs, shaded with vines, and well-made walks, always firm and dry, bordered with shrubbery, or overhung with trees."

Country Home Essentials

George E. Woodward, *Cottages & Farmhouses*, 1867

Easy Stairs

The Register of Rural Affairs,
1873

"Who has not felt discouraged when standing at the foot of a long, straight flight of steps, looking up at that top which must be reached, however tedious and difficult the way may appear?

Put in a landing half or two-thirds up, and a turn in some other direction, and all is changed. The distant goal is hid, as in the journey of life, not seeing very far ahead, we start with confidence, rest a moment perhaps, or change the motion at the turn and reach the top as it were by two efforts, neither of which has been fatiguing. I speak with the more confidence of this matter, as the house we have occupied for years has such a landing, and the ease with which we reach the rooms above is still cause of congratulation, especially after a recent experience in climbing a straight flight. Probably as good proportion as any for steps is 7 1/2 inch riser and 10 inch step. Make the top of second floor exactly 10 feet above the upper side of lower floor, and fifteen of these steps or sixteen risers will land you all right. It is important to make this close calculation before laying the joists, as a single step differing from the rest in height, if only by the fraction of an inch, is exceedingly annoying, and many a serious bruise has been brought about in this way, with perhaps not a suspicion of the cause."

"The sun, if you will only open your house to him, is a faithful physician, who will be pretty constant in attendance, and who will send in no bills. Many years ago glass was something of a luxury, but now we can all have good-sized windows, and plenty of them, at moderate cost, and there is no excuse for making mere loop-holes, through which the sun can cast out half an eye, and from which one can gain only narrow glimpses of the beautiful outer world.

I am sufficiently acquainted with the conservative character of many country people to know that expressions of disdain will come from some quarters when I mention bay windows. Nevertheless bay windows are a good thing. Their effect is very much like letting heaven into one's house, at least it ought to be like that, for it is nothing but absurdity and wickedness to darken such windows with shutters or heavy curtains until only a struggling ray of sunlight can be seen."

"Sunlight in every room of the house is necessary for good health and should be provided for by the location and architecture of the house."

Let the Sun In

E.H.Leland, *Farm Homes*, 1882

Samuel T. Maynard, *Landscape Gardening*, 1899

An 1893 carriage house design from the magazine, *Shoppell's Modern Houses*

Build Backbuildings

One way of spreading the expense of country home construction out over the years is through the use of backbuildings or outbuildings. Yesterday's farmers expanded their farmsteads with specialized buildings for each new crop or product and for each improvement in their life-styles. They built barns, silos, corn cribs, wood sheds, smoke houses, work shops, spring houses, carriage houses, stables and more. Today, you may not need an ice house or outdoor privy, but there is no reason why a home office, studio, library, garage, garden shed, game room or pool house couldn't be built as a separate building.

Build small now, and add to your place as you need it. You'll save cost and, in the end, have a better country place. You'll find that your ideas and needs change over the years. The place that you let evolve over time will work better for you than any building you can imagine now. And, it's usually much easier to add or renovate a small freestanding outbuilding than it is to make substantial changes to a house.

How to Design Outbuildings

This little building, designed in 1867 by architect George E. Woodward, was described by him as a "tool-house, etc." Besides being thankful that we no longer need an outdoor "etc.," we can learn something from the design.

The gingerbread, arched window and roof treatment that you see were a reflection of the same details on the main house. Last century's homeowners knew that by repeating the colors, materials and details of their house on fences and outbuildings, they made the home seem more a part of the land that it was on and improved the look of both.

In order of importance, outbuildings should be built to complement a home by aligning their walls with the house's, by using the same paint and roofing color, by using the same style roof and roof angle, and by using the same details, hardware and such.

A Model Plan

The Register of Rural Affairs, 1857

"This design which represents a house in a nearly square form, gives ten rooms within story and a half walls, the whole measuring only thirty by thirty-five feet inside. The rooms are probably as compactly arranged as can be possibly effected, not a single inch of the enclosed space being lost. The entry, 5 by 7 feet, conducts to the parlor on one side and to the dining-room on the other, the latter being also intended as the family or living-room. The stairs being flanked with plastered walls, are made at one-fourth the expense required where open on one side with railing or balustrade. The entrance to the cellar from the kitchen is under these stairs.

The exterior conveys an expression of cheerfulness and neatness; and has so small an amount of ornamental appendages, that the cost is scarcely increased by them. The window under the small front gable, inserted for lighting the upper hall and stairs, imparts a certain sheltered aspect, which is carried out by the addition of the window hoods over the lower windows."

PRINCIPAL FLOOR.

Hints on Home Plans

A great design can only be built if it is presented clearly to contractors and building officials on a good set of building plans. Here are some ideas on how to find, create or just understand blueprints.

Build on Paper First

E.H.Leland, *Farm Homes,* 1882

"It is a great thing to build the house that is to be one's home. There are few pleasures so unalloyed as that of selecting the ground, laying the foundation, and watching day by day the growth of wall and roof that go to form one's own secure kingdom through the years to come. And it is a pleasure that cannot be entered upon too seriously. If there are to be but three rooms, they will constitute the home, and the opportunity exists to make them either charmingly cozy and cheerful, or depressingly ugly. Therefore, even a small house-plan should be well considered. A house-plan is easily torn down and remodeled; it costs nothing to add a paper window here, or to remove a paper partition there; a pencil line changes a staircase or enlarges the dining-room; a few moments of inexpensive reflection lets the morning sunlight into a cheerless kitchen, builds a clothes-press, and remodels the pantry; or, if something better is thought of, the whole establishment can be easily tossed aside, and not even the shadow of the house-mover's bill presents itself. But, having put a plan into solid timber and mortar, and then coming to find how greatly the house might be improved - ah, woe the day ! It is no idle thing to meddle with the staircases and partitions, and the gloomily-lighted kitchen."

The Features of a Good House Plan

A.W. Brunner, *Cottages, or Hints on Economical Building*, 1884

"A well-studied plan is characterized by compactness and the absence of any visible make-shifts or afterthoughts. Everything fits well and seems in its natural place.

A rectangular house is the cheapest and best, the octagonal and circular forms are better adapted for bays or projections only. Very irregular and straggling plans may product picturesque results, but are sure to be comparatively expensive. A square house has always been a favorite with many practical-minded people. It is such a "sensible" shape and cuts up well into rooms. True, a given length of line, as a square, encloses a greater area than in any other rectangular form, so we get the most house for our materials and money. Still, we will probably find that, after arranging our plan, considering comfort and convenience alone, it will not result in a mathematical square; but, if it be compact and capable of being simply roofed, we need not reproach ourselves with undue extravagance.

All space occupied in passages and corridors, increasing the size but not the capacity of the building, is wasted.

Light and air are, we know, essentials of life. Let us not forget it in planning our house. Dark passages and stairways should not be tolerated."

Prevent Building a Poor Plan

This pretty drawing, on the next page, of an 1849 "English" country cottage by Connecticut architect Gervase Wheeler is just that - a pretty drawing. Look beyond the art of the illustration, and you'll see a far less artful house design.

Look at the figure of the woman on the top step of the entrance, and you'll see a problem. Imagine her standing on the ground. Her head just reaches the bottom of the bay windows. This house is much, much larger than it seems in the illustration. The siding boards are drawn at about two feet wide - much larger than wood siding available now, or then. The artist is tricking us to see this as a "cottage" and not the huge and unnecessarily high house that it really is.

Look at the fillagree and verge boards on the two front gables. Again, they are pretty and were very fashionable in their day. Now, imagine the house without them, when the fashion changed or the owner grew too frustrated at constantly repairing and replacing the fragile boards. Without the decoration, the house will appear unbalanced and unfinished - too many windows below, too few above. The house was designed for its gingerbread, but fads like that last just a few years - homes last and have to look good for hundreds.

Now, look at the plan. The first problem is the predominance of formal rooms. Where can a family get comfortable? The kitchen is too small. The hall is too big. There's no outside door to the kitchen. That's mighty inconvenient when you're carrying groceries. The veranda seems like a nice feature only until you realize that there is no way to reach it without climbing out a window.

Take your time reviewing your plans. Imagine living with the spaces. Draw the paths you'll use most each day right on the floor plan. Compare the distances with the ones you walk now. Look carefully at all sides of the exterior. Are they as nice as the front? Country homes become part of the landscape. They have to be pretty from all views. Sketch people, at the right scale, on each exterior elevation of your design. (Stick figures work fine.) Now, see if the house still looks right. Still in doubt? Paste a blueprint of your elevations onto cardboard and fold them into a rough model. Look at two sides at the same time. That's how you'll see your home it after it's built.

It's far better to invest some time in studying your design than to build a surprise. Make absolutely sure your home is right for you before you build. Miss the season for construction instead of living in an inconvenient house season after season. The cost of mail-order plans is a trifle to the cost of building a home you won't love. And, if you've hired an architect, you're paying for the perfect plan. Make sure you get it.

An "English Cottage"
by Gervase Wheeler,
from *The
Horticulturist*, 1849

Principal Floor Plan

Model Your Plan on a Home You Know

Henry W. Cleaveland, *Village & Farm Cottages,* 1856

"A common mode of procuring a design is to take as a model some house already built. This particularly suits those who experience difficulty in understanding architectural drawings, and in forming the conception of an object, not actually before their eyes. To the copying of a pattern house, if one in all respects suitable can be found, there is perhaps no serious objection, except the sameness. But it is often forgotten that the house which exactly suits its present location and occupants, may seem quite out of place in some other situation, and may be wholly unfit for a different kind of family. If, as often happens, an attempt be made to modify it by altering its proportions, by curtailment in one part, or by some incongruous addition in another, the probability is that the good qualities of the original will be mostly lost, while their few remaining traces will only show the deformity of the alterations.

The same caution is applicable to the selection of published designs. Those principles which should direct in the formation of an original design ought also to control in some degree, at least, the choice of a ready-made plan."

Illustrations of "A Common Country House" and "The Same House Remodelled," from *Woodward's Country Homes,* 1865

"If you are not familiar with all the details of the house you propose to build, make yourself so, by a repeated examination of existing specimens, in dwellings in the same style, already erected. Above all, do not be satisfied by the mere expression on the plan, in figures, of the sizes of your rooms; but ascertain if the size is exactly what you suppose, and what you want, by looking at rooms already built of that size. Otherwise you may find to your regret, when it is too late, that 'parlor 16 by 20' means something a great deal smaller, when actually enclosed within four walls, than it did in the air castle of your imagination, which you conjured up with the aid of your paper plans."

A.J. Downing, *Hints to Persons About Building in the Country*, 1847

Hints on Home Plans

"In planning windows and doors to bedrooms, regard should be had to the importance of locating bedsteads and bureaus with reference to light and drafts, and windows should be arranged accordingly. It is sometimes discovered that the windows have been so injudiciously planned that there is no place for a bed to stand.

An easy way of planning for bedsteads, bureaus, etc., in rooms, is to cut pieces of cardboard of the proper size according to the scale of the rooms. This is usually one fourth inch to the foot. These pieces of card of the exact size of bedsteads, bureaus, buffets, etc., can be moved about on the architect's floor-plan of each room to determine the location of windows, doors, gas-brackets, etc."

Francis C. Moore, *How to Build a Home*, 1897

"Whatever the plan adopted, let it, when once fixed on, be firmly adhered to. Even though it should be found in some slight degree imperfect, attempts to improve it after the work has begun will be more likely to result in injury, loss, and vexation, than in benefit. Those who adopt a published design with the idea of modifying it, should remember that a slight alteration may change its whole character, and destroy its value. Such a change can be safely made only in the same spirit as that which governed in the original formation; and to do it well requires at least equal skill."

Do You Need an Architect?

Henry W. Cleaveland,
Village & Farm Cottages,
1856

"It is an error to suppose that the architect's aid is needed only by those who erect large and expensive houses. The man who in building is compelled to a close economy has, perhaps, even greater occasion for the best professional advice. The architect who is called to plan such a house, and who would make it suitable and satisfactory, must perform a very important duty before he begins to make a drawing. He certainly cannot adapt his plan to the requirements of his employer, until he has ascertained what those requirements are. But so vague, often are the notions of men, that this is no easy matter. They need help to understand and define their own ideas and wishes. In such cases, the architect must explain, and question, and suggest, until his client, as well as himself, shall have a definite notion in regard to the size, accommodation, style, and cost of the proposed erection, and of those paramount considerations to which every thing else must conform. In this matter of advising, an honorable architect will feel his moral responsibility; consulting not so much his own fancy, as the character and true interest of those who are to occupy the dwelling. It will be his aim so to adapt the house to the habits, needs, and circumstances of the family; so to arrange the whole in respect of economy, consistency, and architectural propriety, that the result shall be not only pleasing at first, but from year to year more and more satisfactory."

Samuel T. Maynard,
Landscape Gardening,
1899

"There is, however, a growing taste among our people for amateur architecture which should be encouraged, and many beautiful and well-arranged plans. The pleasure experienced in building a house of one's own planning may more than counterbalance any saving in material or labor that might result from a plan made by a skilled architect."

Popular magazines and plan catalogs offer a great variety of complete construction drawings for country homes. Remember that those drawings are usually made to conform with national standards and may not be just right for your site. You might have to have them adapted for your climate conditions and for special requirements of your local building department and zoning laws.

In all cases, you'll need to have the house sited on your property and a site plan prepared with proper provisions for utilities, septic system, drainage, drives and entrances, landscaping and views. It's always a good idea to consult with a local construction engineer or architect and your building department's engineers before ordering plans.

If you can't find a mail-order plan that's just right, if you find that you're selecting a house that's larger than you need, if your property is steeply sloped, if you have dramatic views that you want to take advantage of, or, if you have special space or site requirements (a darkroom, a pool, a greenhouse or access for someone in a wheelchair, for example), you should consider having a custom home designed. Plan on spending somewhere around 10% of the construction cost for the design fees, allow a few months design time before building and follow the advice on how to select an architect below.

Is a Mail-Order Plan Right for You ?

Choosing an Architect

The House & Home, 1897

"To the selection of a proper architect must be devoted all the experience of a lifetime of observation of men and works. That large class of humble strivers after the right which, for convenience, is broadly designated as the laity, feel their own dependence and inferiority before the professional man, and stand a little in awe of his knowledge, as well as of that adjustable code known as professional etiquette. Throw away such thoughts and regard him not as a superior, to be delicately handled, but as a man whose duty and pleasure it is to serve you.

It is safe to assume that a woman who has kept house intelligently for ten years knows more than any architect about the best practical arrangement of rooms for her family. On that point she should not be too self-effacing."

Can You Build Your Own House ?

A.J. Downing, *Hints to Persons About Building in the Country,* 1847

"Most men in America, who build country houses, are their own 'Clerk of the Works,' that is to say, they undertake to supply the materials, and employ the mechanics; they mostly plan the building, and they take all the general superintendence of the labor. And a sorry time they have of it! If it strengthens patriotism to fight battles for one's country, our amateur builders ought to have a patriotic attachment to their country homes, for many of them have a sore conflict of mind and body from the time they commence building till they bid a joyful adieu to the house-painter.

It does not require much observation to discover the reason of all this difficulty and perplexity. To state it plainly, it is nothing more nor less than the ignorance of the proprietor himself of the whole art of building. Every man does not fancy that he can make a coat, or weave a tapestry, without instruction - yet every man is quite certain that he can not only build a house, but build a much better one, in many respects, than he has seen before, till he has tried! "

Samuel T. Maynard, *Landscape Gardening,* 1899

"It is the almost universal experience of those who build a house for the first time, especially those with limited means, that the cost largely exceeds the estimate, and this has led to the practice of adding twenty-five to fifty percent to the estimate as it is ordinarily made. This deficiency may be accounted for generally by the fact that there are so many little things that go to make up the completed house that are overlooked."

Building Your Country Home

Now comes the hard part - turning design ideas and paper plans into a real house. Here's building advice that's as good today as it was a hundred years ago.

How Much Will the New House Cost?

George E. Woodward, *Cottages and Farm Houses*, 1867

"*A simple and rapid plan for estimating the cost of any building is by comparison. If carefully done, it will give figures that may be relied on. We will suppose that a party desires to erect a building. Let him select such a house already built in that vicinity as shall represent, in style of architecture and character of finish, about what he desires to construct, and of which the cost of building is known; then compute the area or number of square feet covered by the building; divide the number of dollars of cost by the number of square feet thus found, and the price per square foot is ascertained.*

Thus a house 40 feet by 40 feet covers an area of 1,600 square feet; it costs $8,000; and dividing $8,000 by 1,600, shows $5 per square foot. Now what will be the cost of a similar house covering 1,400 square feet? 1,400 x $5 = $7,000.

This plan will do very well to approximate roughly to cost. A better and closer one is to ascertain the cost per cubic foot. Thus, a house 40 feet by 40 feet, and an average height of 30 feet. 40 x 40 x 30 = 48,000 cubic feet, cost $7,200, or fifteen cents per cubic feet. Then a house containing 57,000 cubic feet, at fifteen cents, would cost $8,550. Where all conditions of comparison are equal, such as equal facilities for buying, equal advantages in capital, credit, good management, etc., one can very closely, by this last method, ascertain about the cost of such a building as he proposes to erect."

How to Fix Construction Costs

The House & Home, 1897

"The cost of the proposed work is like the algebraic x, an unknown quantity, unless one of two methods is adopted - and they are open to adverse criticism. To sell a house for thirty thousand dollars one must ask thirty-five for it; to build a house for a prescribed sum one must name to the architect twenty per cent less. It is quite impossible to determine whether it is the ambition of the architect, or the extravagance of his client, or the unstable scale of prices for either labor or materials, which makes this a truism; but certain it is that no one ever yet built within his first-named sum. If time were plenty and years did not count, it could be possible to use the other method of keeping within a certain amount. The architect would then finish his drawings and specifications, from excavations to brass keys, and draw and sign all contracts. Then, by adding the amounts, he would know the entire necessary expenditure. This sounds simple, but experiment has proved it to be almost impracticable, as well as unsatisfactory to the owner, for it makes changes impossible, and few know from drawings what the completed structure will be."

"If the purse is small, let the necessary economy be confined to the elimination of ornament, but never let it tempt the builder to slight the construction of the house. Where there is a choice between showiness and worth, put effect aside, and aim first of all to have the house well constructed of durable, but not extravagant, materials."

Build with Wood

Calvert Vaux, *Villas & Cottages*, 1867

"Pine is undoubtedly a better material than hemlock, yet the latter is much cheaper, and, if of fair quality, is nearly as good for constructive purposes as pine. It is, therefore, quite sufficient in all ordinary buildings to construct the frame, joists, partitions, and roofs of hemlock, using clear pine for the external and internal fittings and finish. Oak is the best, and, in the end, the most economical material to use for heavy timber across wide openings. Chestnut, in short lengths and well supported, is well suited for rough joists or sleepers required for boarded floors close to the earth; and locust-wood, though costly, is invaluable in moist situations for any posts, furring strips, or other wood-work that comes in direct connection with damp basement walls."

George E. Woodward, *Cottages and Farm Houses*, 1867

"A difference of opinion has, and probably always will exist about the materials of which a house should be constructed. We use in this country three leading varieties, wood, brick, and stone, and, to a limited extent, grout and iron. Wood is the cheapest, and if very nice points are considered, is probably the healthiest, certainly the driest. Frame houses have also superior qualities for ventilation, a subject very little understood by those who advocate impenetrable walls and double windows. So little progress has been made in understanding the subject of ventilation, that the commissioners, in advertising for plans for the new Capitol building for the State of New York, mention the necessity of open fire-places for this purpose. Our stone and brick houses, with slate and metal roofs, furnace-heated and air-tight, lack essential qualities for health; while a frame-house, which admits the air more freely, even if it takes an extra cord or two of wood, or an extra supply of coal, has a more healthy atmosphere."

About Your Builders

A.J.Downing, *Hints to Persons About Building in the Country*, 1847

"A good deal of observation and experience has convinced us that building by contract is, in nearly all cases, the better mode in this country. If your master-workman is a man of integrity, he will serve you as faithfully under a fair contract as by the day's-work system, and, if he is not, there is even more likelihood of your being cheated in the latter case than in the former. Letting the work under contract, makes the contractor the only accountable person, and your own supervision is confined to observing that he fulfills the conditions of his contract; and rids you, besides, of the trouble of watching a dozen or twenty subordinates.

There is an opinion strongly maintained by some (and for the indulgence of which they are willing to pay dearly), that good workmanship can only come by the day-work system. We have not found, on comparison of houses built in the different modes, that there is any practical truth in it. Everything, as we have said, depends on the master-workman, and, in this country, if he is allowed a fair compensation for the 'job,' we believe as much justice is always done in one case as the other."

Frances C. Moore, *How to Build a Home*, 1897

"Let no one persuade you to make separate contracts with various contractors - builder, plumber, mason, etc. Unless there is one responsible contractor for the whole work, each of the contractors will plead negligence on the part of one or more of the rest as an excuse for delays. The builder will insist that the mason did not get his foundations finished in time; the plasterer will insist that the roofer did not finish in time for him to commence his work with necessary protection against the weather, etc. Moreover, - and this is a serious matter, - any injury to the building by reason of neglect to protect against the elements will be a matter for which an owner who has various contractors will alone be responsible, whereas if he has one contractor, under obligation to finish and deliver the building in good condition, he will be relieved of protecting the building from storms, washouts, etc., and will also be relieved of the expense of paying watchmen for nights and holidays.

Plenty of time should be given to the various estimating contractors to make their figures, and money will be lost if they are required to estimate without sufficient time for investigation."

A Sway-Back Roof

Leaks

Some Sure Signs of Shoddy Construction

Unexpected Guests
Dropping In

Building Hints

"The top soil is valuable, and should be carefully removed to one side (where it will not be in the way, necessitating subsequent removal), to be readjusted upon the terraces or other surfaces for support of grass, flowers, and other vegetation. It is often foolishly mixed up with the clay and sand, necessitating the purchase afterward of good soil when top dressing is necessary."

"Where the building to be erected is within the jurisdiction of a municipal or State Building Department, it is best to have the plans approved by the department before awarding the contract. This precaution will cost nothing, and may save charges for extra work. If such a clause as the following, 'All work must be done in accordance with the requirements of the Department of Buildings, and any changes in the work made by the order of said department will form a part of this contract, and will be done by the contractor without cost to the owner,' is relied upon to protect the owner, he may rest assured that the contractor will make due allowance in his estimate price for all possibilities, and take the benefit of any doubt, when in fact there need be no doubt."

Frances C. Moore, *How to Build a Home*, 1897

"In building, cheapness is not always true economy. To build without a reasonable regard for strength and durability, merely for the sake of saving, evinces but a short-sighted frugality."

"The question of economy is not a simple geometrical problem, as some would have us consider it. It is not difficult to decide what form of structure will give, with the least amount of material, and at the lowest cost of erection, the greatest quantity of cubic space. Leaving out of the question looks and convenience, the rule might do for a temporary barn, which is to hold nothing but hay; and this is about the extent of its application."

"Spare no pains to obtain the services of honest, intelligent master-mechanics, as deficiencies of construction and execution, and heavy bills of extras, are more frequently the result of dull incapacity and stupid neglect than of a grasping disposition, or of a willful intention to deceive."

Calvert Vaux, *Villas & Cottages*, 1867

How to Communicate with Your Contractor

Henry W. Cleaveland, *Village & Farm Cottages*, 1856

"It is not enough that he who proposes to build should have fully planned the structure, and that all its particulars are distinctly fixed in his own mind. This plan must be made equally clear to the mechanics who are to execute it. It should be so plain as to leave no chance for misunderstanding or perversion. And this requires that all the parts which can be so represented should be shown by drawings made to a scale sufficiently large to admit of measurement by the workmen. Every thing of importance for them to know, which cannot be drawn, should be fully described in writing. Floor-plans, showing the position and dimensions of walls and partitions; elevations, giving the form of each side, with the windows, doors, and other details; framing plans, determining the size and place of each stick of timber to be used; sections of mouldings, cornices, stairs, and all those parts which are of irregular outline; the whole accompanied by careful specifications of the quality of all materials, and the manner of their use,—are not only necessary in order to estimate, before building, what it will cost, hut form the surest safeguard against misunderstandings, and against the taking of wrongful advantage when work is done by contract."

"The scene around buildings in the process of erection is often very disorderly. This may be prevented by a little timely precaution. Let the owner designate, beforehand, places where the various materials shall be deposited, and mark out such space as may be needed for doing the work. The remaining part of the grounds and the trees, if it contains them, may be protected from injury, by a temporary fence. In his agreement with the builder, he should have a provision making him responsible for any damage that may accrue to his own or his neighbor's property through the carelessness or rudeness of the workmen."

"Persons unaccustomed to watch the progress of a building, are liable to be deceived by its appearance in the earlier stages. The rooms look small and seem to be growing smaller, and very few things appear as they supposed they would. Hence often, needless apprehensions and worse than needless complaints. To such, we can only say that they are not competent judges in the case. All that they can do is patiently to await the completion of the structure. By that time, in all probability, their trouble and fears will have vanished."

When the Building Starts

Henry W. Cleaveland, *Village & Farm Cottages*, 1856

Construction Details

TOP RAIL

BALUSTERS

BOTTOM RAIL

TIN LINING
GUTTER

2" X 4" RAFTER

BED MOULDING

CEILING BOARDS
COVE MOULDING

MOULDING

SQUARE

CAPITAL OF COLUMN
ON THE PIAZZA

TOP RAIL

½ STRAIGHT ½ TO TAPER

BALUSTERS

BOTTOM RAIL

PIAZZA FLOOR

Details of Porch Cornice, Column and Rails.—Scale, 1 Inch to the Foot.

"*The owner should require the architect to furnish details of the trim (by which is meant the wood finish, window-frames, door-frames, wash-boards or base-boards, panels under windows, wainscoting, etc.) promptly, - in fact, simultaneously with the plans and other specifications, - in order that the builder may have no excuse for not having all of the trim kiln-dried in time for finishing the building.*

This is a more important matter than at first glance it may appear to be. Builders and contractors are often prevented from finishing their work in time through the negligence of architects in furnishing details, drawings, etc., and do not like to put the blame where it belongs; no builder likes to quarrel with an influential architect. The owner should see that all of the working plans, details, drawings, etc., are fully completed before taking an estimate for the work. He will thus get better prices, because each contractor will know exactly what he has to do, and will not make undue allowance for construction details as to which he may have to guess.

The owner, too, will find it advisable to go over the drawings of the standing trim, doors, patterns of the main staircase, etc., as in case they do not suit him it will be too late to remedy the matter after they have been prepared and brought to the building.

Do not, under any circumstances, consent to have your architect take estimates with the indefinite clause, 'Details hereafter to be furnished'."

Francis C. Moore, *How to Build a Home,* 1897

Finishes & Furnishings

Interior finishes and furniture and exterior materials and colors are an essential part of a country place. Consider these ideas as you plan your new home.

Wainscoting

Someday, when you have nothing better to do, take a yardstick through your house and measure the height, above the floor, of all the finger marks, dents and chipped paint on your walls. You'll find that over 90% of them are lower than that yardstick, and you 'll have discovered why last century's homeowners loved wainscoting.

Any type of wood, stained a natural color and capped between three and four feet high with a "chair-rail," would protect halls, staircases, kitchens and any other well used room. The illustration above, of an 1881 dining room, shows how the chair-rail keeps the weight of a heavy sideboard off the soft plaster wall.

E.H. Leland, *Farm Homes*, 1882

"Walls of kitchens and dining-rooms are generally finished in wood to the height of two and a half or three feet from the floor. This is a good style, not only because it saves the breaking and marring of plaster, but because it gives a look of comfort and solidity to the apartments. Halls, and even parlors, might be finished in the same way, and thus add to the warmth of the house and make wall-papering and other decoration an easier and less expensive operation."

"A point that requires much attention in the study of details is, to make the ornament secondary to the construction, and not the construction secondary to the ornament. This is the fatal rock on which so many a good conception for a house has been split. An inexperienced man, for example, may conclude to have an ornamental plaster-ceiling in his parlor, and in his desire to have it good of its sort, he may so load it down with decoration that it will be much more disagreeable to look at than the plain ceiling was before it was touched. And so it is throughout the whole subject of domestic architecture: it is always as easy to spoil a house by overdoing it as by underdoing it."

Avoid Gewgawgery

Calvert Vaux, *Villas & Cottages*, 1867

"The work should be simple, because cheaper in the first place, in construction, and finish; quite as appropriate and satisfactory in appearance; and demanding infinitely less labor and pains to care for, and protect it afterward. Therefore all mouldings, architraves, chisel-work, and gewgawgery in interior finish should be let alone in the living and daily occupied rooms of the house. If, to a single parlor, or spare bed chamber a little ornamental work be permitted, let even that be in moderation, and just enough to teach the active mistress and her daughters what a world of scrubbing and elbow work they have saved themselves in the enjoyment of a plainly-finished house, instead of one full of gingerbread work and finery."

Lewis F. Allen, *Rural Architecture*, 1852

Hints on Home Materials

The Register of Rural Affairs, 1855, 1856 & 1857

"Build of such good materials as are near at hand. An interesting index is afforded to the resources and materials of that particular region, with the addition of great economy over the use of such as are 'far brought and dear bought'."

"Prefer lasting to perishable materials, even more costly. A small well built erection, is better than a large decaying shell."

"Discard all gingerbread work, and adopt a plain, neat, and tasteful appearance in every part. Far more true taste is evinced by proper forms and just proportions than by any amount of tinsel and peacock decorations. A marble statue bedizened with feathers and ribbons, would not be a very pleasing object."

Outside Finishes

Calvert Vaux, *Villas & Cottages*, 1867

"The ordinary mode of horizontal siding seems preferable in most situations. It offers a simple, fair surface, that can be broadly treated both in form and color, for the slight projection of one board over the other does not give sufficient variety of light and shade to interfere with the general effect as a whole. Another method is to groove and tongue the boards together, and bring all to one smooth surface. This plan has nothing to recommend it; it is more costly, more likely to get out of order by expansion and contraction, and is scarcely more agreeable in appearance. It is possible, instead of using siding, to cover a building with shingles, and to cut them into ornamental patterns. And this was often done by the Dutch settlers; but the projection is so slight, that not much additional effect is gained, except, perhaps, in quite small buildings, for the impression that a residence of tolerable size makes on the eye depends very little on such merely superficial detail.

Another plan is to use vertical boarding, with battens to cover the joints, for an external covering. This mode has some advantages, and its appearance is often preferred. It is well suited for barns or small buildings, where the battens are relatively large enough to form part of the design; but when used on a larger scale, it is apt to give a striped, liny appearance to a house that injures its broad, general effect, and to draw particular attention to the fact that it is built of wood. This fact should not in any way be denied; but it is not desirable to make it especially prominent, as if it was something to be particularly proud of."

E.H. Leland, *Farm Homes*, 1882

"For covering roofs of houses in the country there is scarcely any good material so generally available as shingles, if the pitch is not too flat. The great advantage of a shingle roof is, that it is scarcely possible for it to get out of order till the wood absolutely rots; and this takes many years to accomplish if the shingles are tolerable and the work well done. It also allows of considerable expansion, contraction, and even settlement, without the slightest injury to its efficiency. It is agreeably varied in surface, and assumes, by age, a soft, pleasant, neutral tint that harmonizes with any color that may be used in the building. A shingle roof in cities, or even closely-built villages, is objectionable in case of fire, because the loose, lighted chips from an adjacent burning building will be likely to inflame it. But this objection does not amount to much in a detached building in the country."

Should Your Country Home be White?

Vick's Monthly Magazine, 1881

"It seems almost unnecessary to allude to the custom of painting houses white, but the practice is yet continued with pertinacity, as if the highest idea of beauty was reached in a white house with green blinds. Riding along our village and country roads, white houses, reflecting the rays of a bright sun, will glare at us on every side, until the sense is absolutely pained, and relief is sought by closing the eyes. These places are often without a particle of shade of trees or vines. To be sure, it takes time to raise trees, but many of the houses could be absolutely transformed by the expenditure of a single dollar for climbing vines, and affording them the proper care in raising and training them. It makes no difference with the seasons in regard to white houses, for if the sun shines less brightly or is obscured by clouds in winter, it is probable that, at the north, the ground will be covered with snow, between which and the house there is no contrast, but all is an unbroken field of white. There is no excuse for such shocking displays of bad taste, and with all the attention that is being given to art by our young people, it is to be hoped that this feature of our early development will soon be lost."

Calvert Vaux, *Villas & Cottages*, 1867

"The question of color is a most interesting one in any design for a country house, and seems at present but little understood in America, by far the greater number of houses being simply painted white, with bright green blinds. By this means each residence is distinctly protruded from the surrounding scenery, and instead of grouping and harmonizing with it, asserts a right to carry on a separate business on its own account; and this lack of sympathy between the building and its surroundings is very disagreeable to an artistic eye. Even a harsh, vulgar outline may often pass without particular notice in a view of rural scenery, if the mass is quiet and harmonious in color; while a very tolerable composition may injure materially the views near it if it is painted white, the human eye being so constituted that it will be constantly held in bondage by this striking blot of crude light, and compelled to give it unwilling attention.

In some cases, the house-painters themselves show a laudable desire to escape from monotonous repetition; but, on the other hand, they are often very troublesome opponents to reform in this matter. And this is not to be wondered at; for a mechanic who has been brought up on a chalk-white and spinach-green diet ever since he was old enough to handle a brush, can hardly help having but little taste for delicate variety, because a perpetual contemplation of white lead and verdigris is calculated to have the same effect on the eye that incessant tobacco-chewing has on the palate: in each case the organ is rendered incapable of nice appreciation."

Fashionable New York city architects and editors like Vaux and James Vick railed against country folks' love of white houses. But, farmers praised the benefits in their journals. White paint was considered "neighborly" by continuing the country tradition; it protected wood because it reflected the sun; it extended the work day by brightening the door yard at dusk. Because it was a simple mix of white lead and linseed oil, new white paint always matched the old. Extensions were easy to finish, and homes could be repainted one side at a time.

Follow Nature's Color Scheme

The Horticulturist, 1847

"No one is successful in rural improvements, who does not study nature, and take her for the basis of his practice. Now, in natural landscape, any thing like strong and bright colors is seldom seen, except in very minute portions, and least of all pure white—chiefly appearing in small objects like flowers. The practical rule which should be deduced from this, is, to avoid all these colors which nature avoids. In buildings, we should copy those that she offers chiefly to the eye—such as those of the soil, rocks, wood, and the bark of trees,—the materials of which houses are built. These materials offer us the best and most natural study from which harmonious colors for the houses themselves should be taken.

Country houses, thickly surrounded by trees, should always be painted of a lighter shade than those standing exposed. And a new house, entirely unrelieved by foliage, as it is rendered conspicuous by the very nakedness of its position, should be painted several shades darker than the same building if placed in a well wooded site. In proportion as a house is exposed to view, let its hue be darker, and where it is much concealed by foliage, a very light shade of color is to be preferred."

The Value of Old Furniture

George E. Woodward, *Cottages and Farm Houses*, 1867

"We have a decided penchant for all that smacks of antiquity. We like old houses and old furniture, particularly if comely and serviceable. We delight in painting to ourselves the scenes through which they must have passed; we believe, too, that they exert a much greater influence in producing a love for home than those constructed at a more recent period.

We would gladly see the money now expended in the trashy, half-made articles of furniture, merely because the uncomfortable shapes of some of them are said to be of the latest style, laid out for those which are truly strong and serviceable, and, for this reason, elegant."

"How rarely does one find really comfortable chairs anywhere? People seem to buy the style of furniture in fashion at the time, and this is usually made with a greater regard to show, than to comfort. In the country, where hard working men and women need easy and restful seats, there seems to be a great lack of them. The best room may have some hair-covered or rep-covered rocking or lounging chairs, but these are too good for daily use, by tired people in their working clothes, and as for taking the best furniture out of doors, that is not to be thought of. We Americans, especially those of us who live in the country, make but very little use of our spacious summer parlor -"all out doors" A wide spreading tree, a vine covered arbor, a broad veranda or porch, and awning like a huge umbrella, or a tent with no sides or even an open shed is a much more comfortable place for sewing, reading, and resting, than any place in-doors, and often comes handy for ironing and other work. For the enjoyment of the open air in any case, seats and chairs that are not too good for rough usage or too rough for ease are needed. The good old-fashioned framed chairs, with split-wood or flagged seats, have long been discarded for the glued work of the modern cabinet maker, but we are glad to see them coming into use again; they were formerly the regular furniture of the farm house; now they are offered as luxuries at the fashionable furnishing stores, and are purchased by those city persons who go into the country for the summer, and wish to take some strong comfortable chairs with them."

Have Comfortable Chairs

The American Agriculturist, 1874

Interior Woodwork

A.W. Brunner, *Cottages or Hints on Economical Building*, 1884

"For door and window trims and other interior woodwork, white pine is recommended, as it is the cheapest, and, if properly finished, looks very well. It may be stained, if too light—the transparent stains merely darken the wood and do not conceal the natural grain. Under no circumstances try to imitate oak or walnut by graining. Such shams deceive no one and are in the worst taste. If we use paint for interior work let us use it frankly, carefully selecting the color, and avoiding a shiny surface, a flatted or dull finish being preferable."

"The interior woodwork should be selected with some little care, and all stained - either satin-wood or light black-walnut. These stains, which can be easily procured, are better if laid on in oil, and then, if covered with two coats of varnish, make the nearest approach possible to the appearance of the above-named natural woods. No grainer's art can do as well. Handsomely stained and varnished woodwork is, we think, the most superior mode of treating interiors. It adds much to the warmth and cosiness of the rooms, has the effect of furnishing, and, so far as cleanliness is concerned, is of great help to the housekeeper. This style of finish, whether for the humble cottage or costly mansion, is better and more attractive, if done with good taste, than the most costly and elaborately painted tints."

"Plants, whether upon a stand or hanging in appropriate pots at the window, add amazingly to the cheerfulness of any room, contributing to the pleasure of those who care and tend for them. They serve also as useful barometers, telling us, by their condition, of the atmospherical state of our apartments, their delicate organization being unable to stand against the injurious emanation from overheated furnaces. Mr. Rand, in his pleasant book upon flowers, says, A plant or a stand of flowers is a constant source of pleasure in a room; it is a spring of sunshine, and its silent influence makes all the household more cheerful and better."

Have Houseplants

George E. Woodward, *Cottages & Farm Houses*, 1867

" A good house: but the home is only half built."

Complete Your Country Home

Isaac Phillips Roberts, *The Farmstead*, 1900

"A house and a home."

Landscaping
Your Country Place

After construction, the property around your buildings will look
stark and barren. Work with nature, as the old-timers did, and you'll
have a lush, easy-to-maintain landscape in a season.

Don't Let This Happen to You!

A.J. Downing, *Hints to Persons About Building in the Country,* 1847

"It is not an uncommon spectacle to see a country house built at a lavish expenditure, and in a very ornate style, but placed in the midst of grounds badly laid out and wretchedly kept. The proprietor has exhausted all his forced stock of enthusiasm, and spent all his surplus capital upon his villa, in his architectural fever, and his grounds are doomed to suffer the succeeding ague of indifference and neglect. A wise man, when he plans a country residence, will so apportion his means that his house may not be out of keeping with his grounds. The same style, the same feeling, should pervade both, and be reflected from one to the other."

"There is a grand error which many fall into in building, looking as they do only at the extent of wood and timber, or stone and mortar in the structure, and paying no attention to the surroundings, which in most cases contribute more to the effect of the establishment than the structure itself, and which, if uncultivated or neglected, any amount of expenditure in building will fail to give that completeness and perfection of character which every homestead should command.

Trees properly distributed, give a value to an estate far beyond the cost of planting, and tending their growth, and which no other equal amount of labor and expense upon it can confer. Innumerable farms and places have been sold at high prices, over those of perhaps greater producing value, merely for the trees which embellished them. Thus, in a pecuniary light, to say nothing of the pleasure and luxury they confer, trees are a source of profitable investment.

If the planter feels disposed to consult authorities, as to the best disposition of his trees, works on Landscape Gardening may be studied; but these can give only general hints, and the only true course is to strive to make his grounds look as much like nature herself as possible—for nature seldom makes mistakes in her designs."

A Good Investment

Lewis F. Allen, *Rural Architecture*, 1852

Make Your Home a Part of the Landscape

Lewis F. Allen, *Rural Studies*, 1852

"A farm with its buildings, or a simple country residence with the grounds which enclose it, or a cottage with its door-yard and garden, should be finished sections of the landscape of which it forms a part. A dwelling house, no matter what the style, standing alone, either on hill or plain, apart from other objects, would hardly be an attractive sight. As a mere representation of a particular style of architecture, or as a model of imitation, it might excite our admiration, but it would not be an object on which the eye and the imagination could repose with satisfaction.

But assemble around that dwelling subordinate structures, trees, and shrubbery properly disposed, and it becomes an object of exceeding interest and pleasure in the contemplation."

A.J. Downing, *Hints to Persons About Building in the Country*, 1847

"The beauty of a cottage or villa, like all beauty of a higher kind, is, we think, much enhanced by a due concealment, rather than a bold display of its attractions. Gleaming through a veil of soft green foliage, we are led to magnify its charms, from there being something pleasing suggested, which is not seen. If, on the contrary, we see the whole building studiously exposed, and that but too often in the broad sunshine, we are only inclined to turn away in disappointment."

Calvert Vaux, *Villas & Cottages*, 1857

"The great charm in the forms of natural landscape lies in its well-balanced irregularity. This is also the secret of success in every picturesque village, and in every picturesque garden, country-house, or cottage."

Carefree Country Planting

"Most men go to the country to make an easy thing of it. If they must commence study of all the later discoveries in vegetable physiology, and keep a sharp eye upon all new varieties of fruit - lest they fall behind the age; and trench their land every third year, and screen it - may be - in order to ensure the most perfect condition of the soil, they find themselves entering upon the labors of a new profession, instead of lightening the fatigues of an old one.

Limit yourself, until you have felt your way, to some ten or a dozen of the best established varieties; don't be afraid of old things if they are good; if a gaunt Rhode Island Greening tree is struggling in your hedge-row, trim it, scrape it, soap it, dig about it, pull away the turf from it, lime it, and then if you can keep up a fair fight against the bugs and the worms, you will have fine fruit from it; if you can't, cut it down. If a veteran mossy pear tree is in your door-yard, groom it as you would a horse - just in from a summering in briary pastures.

Save some sheltered spot for a trellis, where you may plant a Delaware, an Iona or two, a Rebecca, and a Diana. Put a Concord at your southside door - its rampant growth will cover your trellised porch in a pair of seasons; it will give you some fine clusters, even though you allow it to tangle; the pomologists will laugh at you; but let them: you will have your shade and the wilderness of frolicsome tendrils, and at least a fair show of purple bunches. Scatter here and there hardy herbaceous flowers that shall care for themselves, and which the children may pluck with a will. Don't distress yourself if your half acre of lawn shows some hummocks, or dandelions, or butter-cups. And if a wild clump of bushes intrude in a corner, don't condemn it too hastily; it may be well to enliven it with an evergreen or two - to dig about it, and paint its edges with a few summer phloxes or roses."

Donald G. Mitchell, *Rural Studies*, 1867

E.H. Leland, *Farm Houses*, 1882

"Beautiful are the ways of the Vine, whether it be the bold and vigorous Virginia Creeper, that finds foothold on the most forbidding wall, and grows the stronger and greater for the winds and storms that beat upon it, or the light and delicate Smilax, weaving its emerald-green tracery across the window panes, or around the portraits of beloved friends.

The forests are full of beautiful vines. Convolvulus, Bitter Sweet, Scarlet, and Yellow Honeysuckle, Virgin's Bower, Grape, and other graceful wild climbers, are within the reach of almost every country house, and should be sought after and wooed to grow around porches, and over gateways, and up on the roofs of unlovely sheds.

The Hop is a wholesome, thrifty vine, and if none other could be had, I would gladly and gratefully train it over verandas, and across kitchen and pantry windows, and rejoice in its cool shade and clean fragrance. But whoever has the good luck to live near a bit of wild woodland, can be generally sure of finding many things that will add grace and beauty to the plainest little home."

Vick's Monthly Magazine, 1886

"Beautiful effects can be produced by the judicious planting and training of hardy climbing plants about the house, and with especial reference to the ornamentation of entrance porches and verandas, and this feature of ornamental gardening should receive more general attention than is given to it. It can be done without the aid of the professional gardener, though we should, by all means, have his assistance, if possible, for the trained mind and the skilled hand are as capable of exhibiting their superiority in garden work as in any other art. But, even without such assistance, one who appreciates beauty and loves nature cannot fail with such materials as thrifty-growing and gracefully climbing and trailing plants, to produce effects that are pleasing to the eye."

Decorate Your Home with Vines

The American Agriculturist, 1877

"If home-makers look after no other portion of the gardening, they are quite sure to take an interest, in the vines, which cluster so closely around the door and windows, that they seem a part of the house rather than of the garden. Here is a common ground on which all can meet - the decoration of the house, for there is no work of the architect, however costly, but seems to need the final finish of vines, and no house, however poor in its exterior, but may be made to look home-like by the use of climbers. In our climate every house should have a veranda of some sort, even if but a mere porch, to shelter the door, and whether it be an extended veranda or narrow "stoop," there is a place for vines. The utility of vines, whether on the score of shade, or that of mere ornament, needs no showing, as all will admit it, and it becomes merely a question of ways and means - what to plant, and how to get it. Let us also say that if there is neither veranda or porch, and most log houses, and some houses of more pretensions have neither, one need not be without vines. A trellis of poles of some kind can be arranged to support the vines, and if it can be made of cedar and permanent, all the better, but if this can not be commanded, draw upon the stock of bean-poles, or get poles by some means that will answer for a season. No matter if it looks rude at first, the vines will charitably cover any sins of construction."

Don't Over-Do Your Landscape

The Horticulturist Magazine, 1865

"*Landscape gardening in a door-yard often verges upon the ridiculous. The proprietor, having read the standard authors, or visited a few large country residences, is seized with the rural fever, and determines to try his hand at improving his own place. He forthwith draws up a plan, with its winding walks and roads, its summer-houses, pines, oaks, magnolias, flower-patches, and what not. Large package of trees and shrubs and vines are ordered from the nursery, and groups and masses and screens are set out all in a grand way. The work looks very fine to the owner; but to any discerning eye that stops to forecast the future, the little plat looks crowded and overburdened before it is half planted. A few years roll by, and how does the place look to everybody? It is one great confused mass of foliage, the trees overgrowing each other, and kill-*

ing out the grass and shrubs beneath. Even the planter himself is dissatisfied, and wishes he had never meddled with landscape gardening.

The obvious lesson from cases like this is that in small places only a few trees should be planted. These should be set along the boundaries, near the gates, and at wide intervals over the surface. Calculate their spread for twenty years or more to come, and plant accordingly. It is often said, we are aware, the trees may be set close together at first for immediate effect, with the design of removing a portion of them when they become crowded. This is all very well if that intention is faithfully carried out; but in most cases it is not. The owner dislikes to cut down the trees which he has planted, or he neglects to do so until they have grown up tall and gaunt, like those of a forest."

"Some beginners dot their lawn over with new-fangled trees, or crowd it with vases and statuary, or arbors, rustic seats and rock-work, or they throw it into jolting terraces, or cut it up into flower-beds in arabesque patterns. I remember a lawn of moderate dimensions in which there are six cast iron vases, two lions, four dogs, four female figures representing the Seasons, besides several other works in terra-cotta. This is the classical run mad. On the same street is another lawn, much smaller, in which a great number of the new weeping trees are huddled together. This is nature made awry, and the distortion makes the beholder uncomfortable. A single specimen of these oddities may sometimes be set on the side of a lawn, for variety, and just to show what nature and art can do, but more than one is too many."

"If landscape gardeners would always bear in mind that generally the simplest airs have the richest harmonies, that simplest subjects make the grandest pictures, and simplest designs make the most pleasing pleasure grounds, we would not be offended by so many strained, formal and unnatural garden effects. If they would use simpler lines and curves, and pay greater attention to fixing the places for permanent trees, they would produce much more charming effects. In small pleasure grounds avoid straight lines, in kitchen gardens avoid curves."

Blanket Your Home with Evergreens

The Register of Rural Affairs, 1866

"Many land-owners, who have a more distinct appreciation of dollars and cents, than of the beauties of nature, cannot see the propriety of occupying ground and labor in setting out ornamental trees. To such, as well as to all others, we wish to urge the importance of planting evergreen trees as a shelter against the cold winds of winter. We once knew a country resident who flanked his house on the sides of prevailing winds with groups and masses of evergreens, from the neighboring forests and borders of swamps - and drew upon himself pretty freely the jeers of his neighbors, for setting out trees that 'bore nothing to eat,' and were 'only good to look at.' In the course of years however, when these trees had attained a height of some twenty feet, and had afforded ample shelter from the winds that swept across the bleak hill occupied by his dwelling, the neighbors discovered that the place had become decidedly more comfortable in cold weather - also that many dollars in firewood were annually saved by the beautiful and efficient protection afforded. They began to see new charms in ornamental trees, and were disposed to adopt what they had once ridiculed."

Use Your Axe

Donald G. Mitchel, *Rural Studies*, 1867

"Most planters about a country home are too much afraid of the axe; yet judicious cutting is of as much importance as planting; and I have seen charming thickets shoot up into raw, lank assemblage of boles of trees without grace or comeliness, for lack of courage to cut trees at the root. For all good effects of foliage in landscape gardening - after the fifth year - the axe is quite as important an implement as the spade."

"*One of the greatest and commonest errors in tree-planting, is that of setting out large trees and many .of them, in small areas. The home improver thinks that he wants a great variety of trees, such as he has seen on Mr. Smith's place, and at Judge Jones' great establishment. So he adds tree to tree, year after year. While they are small, they look pretty, and all goes on well. But ere long, they spread out their limbs on every side, until they meet and overlap each other, making a complete forest jungle. None of them can become well-formed trees; they grow up spindling, or lop-sided, and give little real satisfaction. And besides, what can be expected of the grass under such overhanging boughs and such a mass of tree-roots? And what of shrubs and plants? Where, too, are the views of the street, or of the surrounding country? Everyway, the practice is bad.*

Here let a remedy be suggested: Set out but few trees. Plant the largest along the boundaries, and the smaller around the dwelling. Set them so as to preserve views of the neighborhood, at the best out-looks. Calculate for their growth many years ahead, and plant accordingly. Many persons plant a large number of trees in their grounds, intending, at some future day, when the trees become crowded, to thin them out. But very few persons have resolution enough to cut down a tree which has become large and thrifty, especially if it was planted by themselves."

Avoid This Mistake

The American Agriculturist, 1862

Make sure to plan on how big your trees will be after they've grown.

Let Time Decorate Your Home

George E. Woodward, *Cottages and Farm Houses*, 1867

"Time, in its many changes, adds beauty and value to a country home that is taken care of, whose occupants enjoy and are interested in every tree and shrub, and every improvement that is made. Fruits, flowers, and ornamental foliage develop new attractions; and a little done to-day, and a little to-morrow, while being but healthful recreation, amounts to a good deal at the end of a year."

Never Finish Your Landscape

Donald G. Mitchell, *Rural Studies*, 1867

"It is a mistake to aim at the completion of a country home in a season, or in two, or some half a dozen. Its attractiveness lies, or should lie, in its prospective growth of charms. Your city home - when once the architect, and plumber, and upholsterer have done their work - is in a sense complete, and the added charms must lie in the genial socialities and hospitalities with which you can invest it; but with a country home, the fields, the flowers, the paths, the hundred rural embellishments, may be made to develop a constantly recurring succession of attractive features. This year, a new thicket of shrubbery, or a new gate-way on some foot-path; next year, the investment of some out-lying ledge with floral wonders; the season after may come the establishment of a meadow (by judicious drainage) where some ugly marsh has offended the eye; and the succeeding summer may show the redemption of the harsh briary up-land that you have scourged into fertility and greenness."

Source Books

Allen, Lewis F. 1852. *Rural Architecture.* New York: C.M. Saxton Agricultural Book Publisher.

Atwood, Daniel T. 1871. *Atwood's Country and Suburban Houses.* New York: Orange Judd & Co.

Bailey, L.H. 1898. *Garden Making: Suggestions for the Home Grounds.* Norwood, MA: The Norwood Press.

Baker, Z. 1857. *Modern House Builder.* Boston: Higgins Bradley and Dayton.

Bicknell, Amos J. 1874. *Bicknell's Village Builder & Supplement.* New York: A.J.Bicknell & Co.

_____, ed. 1875. *Wooden and Brick Buildings with Details.* New York: A.J.Bicknell & Co.

_____. 1879. *Specimen Book of One Hundred Architectural Designs.* New York: A.J. Bicknell & Co.

Brunner, Arnold W., ed. 1884. *Cottages or Hints on Economical Building.* New York: William T. Compstock.

Carleton, Will. 1873. *Farm Ballads.* New York: Harper Brothers.

_____. 1875. *Farm Legends.* New York: Harper Brothers.

_____. 1885. *City Ballads.* New York: Harper Brothers.

Cleaveland, Henry W., William Backus and Samuel D. Backus. 1856. *Village and Farm Cottages.* New York: Appleton Co.

Comstock, William T., ed. 1881. *Comstock's Modern Architectural Designs and Details.* New York: William T. Comstock.

_____. 1883. *American Cottages.* New York: William T. Comstock.

Downing, Andrew Jackson. 1841. *A Treatise on the Theory and Practice of Landscape Gardening.* New York: Wiley & Putnam.

_____. 1842. *Cottage Residences.* New York: Wiley & Putnam.

_____. 1847. *Hints to Persons about Building in the Country.* New York: Wiley & Putnam.

_____. 1850. *The Architecture of Country Houses.* New York: D. Appleton & Co.

_____. 1853. *Rural Essays.* New York: G.P. Putnam & Co.

Fowler, Orson Squire. 1848. *A Home for All: or The Gravel Wall and Octagon Mode of Building.* New York: Fowlers and Wells.

Halstead, Byron D. 1881. *Barn Plans and Outbuildings.* New York: Orange Judd Co.

Harney, George E. 1870. *Barns, Outbuildings and Fences.* New York: The American News Company.

Hill, Thomas E. 1880. *Hill's Manual of Social and Business Forms.* Chicago: Hill Standard Book Co.

Hobbs, Isaac H. and Son. 1876. *Hobbs's Architecture.* Philadelphia: J.B.Lippincott & Co.

Holly, Henry Hudson. 1866. *Holly's Country Seats.* New York: Appleton & Co.

Hussey, Elisha Charles. 1875. *Home Building.* New York: Leader & Van Hoesen.

Jacques, Daniel Harrison. 1866. *The House: A Manual of Rural Architecture.* New York: George Woodward.

King, David W. 1885. *Homes for Home Builders.* New York: Orange Judd Co.

Leland, E.H. 1882. *Farm Homes In-doors and Out-doors.* New York: Orange Judd Co.

Maynard, Samuel T. 1899. *Landscape Gardening.* New York: John Wiley & Sons.

Mitchell, Donald Grant. 1867. *Rural Studies.* New York: Charles Scribner & Co.

Moore, Frances C. 1897. *How to Build a Home.* New York: Doubleday & McClure Co.

Munkittrick, Richard Kendall. 1891. *Farming.* New York: Harper & Brothers.

Reed, Samuel Burrage. 1878. *House Plans for Everybody.* New York: Orange Judd Co.

_____. 1883. *Cottage Houses.* New York: Orange Judd Co.

Roberts, Isaac Phillips. 1900. *The Farmstead.* New York: MacMillan Company.

Robinson, Solon. 1863. *Facts for Farmers.* New York: A.H.Johnson.

Scott, Frank J. 1870. *Suburban Home Grounds.* New York: D. Appleton & Co.

Shoppell, Robert W., ed. 1883. *How to Build, Furnish & Decorate.* New York: Co-operative Building Plan Association.

Sloan, Samuel. 1852. *The Model Architect.* Philadelphia: E.S.Jones & Co.

_____. 1866. *Sloan's Homestead Architecture.* Philadelphia: J.B.Lippincott & Co.

Todd, Sereno Edwards. 1860. *The Young Farmer's Manual.* New York: C.M.Saxon, Barker & Co.

_____. 1888. *Todd's Country Homes or Winning Solid Wealth.* Philadelphia: Hubbard Bros.

Vaux, Calvert. 1857. *Villas and Cottages.* New York: Harper & Brothers.

Wheeler, Gervase. 1851. *Rural Homes.* New York: Charles Scribner.

_____. 1855. *Homes for the People in Suburb and Country.* New York: Charles Scribner.

Wicks, William S. 1889. *Log Cabins and Cottages, How to Build and Furnish Them.* New York: Forest & Stream Co.

Wightwick, George. and Andrew Jackson Downing. 1847. *Hints to Young Architects.* New York: Wiley & Putnam.

Woodward, George E. 1865. *Woodward's Country Homes.* New York: George E. & F.W. Woodward.

_____. 1866. *Architecture, Landscape Gardening and Rural Art, No. I.* New York: George E. & F.W.Woodward.

_____. 1867. *Architecture and Rural Art, No. II.* New York: George E. Woodward.

_____. 1867. *Cottages and Farmhouses.* New York: The American News Company.

19th Century Magazine, Almanac & Farm Journal Sources

The American Agriculturist.
The American Magazine.
Arthur's Ladies' Magazine.
The Breeder's Gazette.
Carpentry & Building.
The Country Gentleman.
The Cultivator.
Genessee Farmer.
Godey's Lady's Book.
Harper's New Monthly Magazine.
The Homestead.
The Horticulturist.
House & Home.
The New England Farmer.
Ohio Farmer.
Peals Popular Educator.
Peterson's Magazine.
Prarie Farmer.
The Register of Rural Affairs.
The Rural American.
The Rural New Yorker.
Shoppell's Modern Houses.
The Southern Cultivator.
Vick's Monthly Magazine.

Index

The American Agriculturist,
1862

"We might add other hints, but these are all that our crowded col-umns will now admit. To all contemplating building dwelling houses, we say, think twice before you build once."

About the Editor   Don Berg, a member of the American Institute of Architects and the Society of Architectural Historians, has published fifteen books on American building and landscape design, including the new book *American Country Building Design*, from Sterling Publishing. His designs and articles have appeared in *Home Magazine, The Old House Journal, Hudson Valley Magazine, Yankee Home* magazine and many other publications. He has lectured on folk architecture at the Museum of American Folk Art and appeared in the TV special *The American Farmhouse* on the Home and Garden Network.

Also from
Donald J. Berg, AIA:

BARNS AND BACKBUILDINGS: Designs for Barns, Carriage Houses, Stables, Garages & Sheds, with Sources for Building Plans, Books, Timber Frames, Kits, Hardware, Cupolas & Weather Vanes.

Edited by Donald J. Berg
96p, 8 1/2 x 11, paperback, ISBN 0-9663075-0-X, $9.95

"Charming Outbuildings" - *The Baltimore Sun*

If you're planning to build in your backyard, you need this book. It has 94 variations of designs for barns, stables, carriage houses, craft barns, garages, workshops, studios, sheds, playhouses and garden structures. You'll find plans, kits, timber frames and prefabricated structures. You'll also find some common sense advice on planning and building on your property.

Rebuild a historic, hundred year old timber frame barn on your property and preserve part of America's rural heritage. Have a new frame built just for you. Find the architect or designer who can create a custom building for your special needs. Find the mail-order plan that's just right and then add a pre-built cupola, hand forged hardware and a weather vane custom made just for you. Now, you have the sources to turn your property into the perfect country place.

"A must book if you are planning the construction of a small barn" - Charles Leik, Editor, *The Barn Journal On-Line.*

Barns & Backbuildings is available from all major on-line bookstores, at bookshops, or by mail from: Donald J. Berg, AIA, PO Box 698, Rockville Centre, NY 11571. Please send $9.95 plus $3 for postage & handling.